THE A TO Z OF BOXING

Written by

Clyde Prisk & Lara Dearnley

THE A TO Z OF BOXING

This edition first published in the UK in 2009
By Green Umbrella Publishing

www.gupublishing.co.uk

Publishers Jules Gammond and Vanessa Gardner

Printed and bound in Italy

ISBN: 978-1-906635-30-5

Contents

Ali

▶ Cassius Clay, as Ali was known when he won Olympic gold in 1960.

▶▶ Henry Cooper flooring Ali with his trademark left hook.

It is, perhaps, fitting that this A-Z begins with the pugilist who is best known to those who are keen followers of boxing, as well as those who merely have a passing interest and even those who have no love for two men battering each other in the name of sport. Muhammad Ali – the self-proclaimed "Greatest" – captured the public's imagination like no other before him during the 1960s and 1970s. With catchphrases like "Float like a butterfly, sting like a bee", Ali became the housewives' favourite.

Born Cassius Marcellus Clay in Louisville, Kentucky, on 17 January 1942, Ali gave up his "slave name" when he joined the Nation of Islam in 1964, first becoming "Muhammad X". He turned professional in 1960, the same year he won the light heavyweight gold medal at the Olympics in Rome and quickly established himself as one of the greatest fighters of all time with the speed of his hands and his nimble feet.

Within four years, he had won the world heavyweight title with a surprise victory over Sonny Liston, but it almost didn't happen as Ali survived a scare when he was unceremoniously dumped on the canvas by British hopeful Henry Cooper in June 1963. The fight with Liston, however, was not without controversy. Ali's corner claimed that his opponent came out for the fourth round with something on his gloves that temporarily blinded the challenger. As

it was, Ali managed to clear his vision and, when the bell rang to signal the start of the seventh round, Liston retired claiming an injured shoulder. Many were sceptical, but doubts were cast aside in the rematch when Ali knocked his opponent out in the first round.

Ali remained undefeated until losing on points to Joe Frazier in what has been called the Fight of the Century in March 1971, although he had been suspended from boxing between 1967 and 1970 because of his refusal to serve in Vietnam. Ali went on to participate in numerous famous fights, including the Rumble in the Jungle against George Foreman (October 1974) where he won the WBA and WBC heavyweight titles, and the Thrilla in Manilla which saw Ali and Frazier clash for a third time. Leon Spinks ended his reign in February 1978 but Ali became the first man to win the title three times when he won the rematch seven months later.

Ali came out of retirement to fight Larry Holmes and Trevor Berbick in the early 1980s but was a shadow of his former self. He was diagnosed with Parkinson's disease in 1984 but remains a much loved celebrity and lit the flame at the 1996 Atlanta Olympics.

Armstrong

▼ Henry Armstrong posing with Petey Sarron.

Born in Columbus, Mississippi, on 12 December 1912, Henry Melody Jackson found fame and fortune under the name Henry Armstrong. Nicknamed "Homicide Hank", Armstrong was the first boxer to simultaneously hold world titles at three different weights.

Brought up in St Louis, he soon discovered his talent and began fighting, more often than not, selling the trophies he won to help feed his family. But he fell in with the wrong crowd and found himself being paid to dictate the outcome of fights according to the wishes of crooked gamblers and mobsters.

His professional career began – with a name change to hide his history – at the age of 18 with a third round defeat at the hands of Al Lovino, but he found his feet in the ring and won his first world title with a sixth round knockout of featherweight champion Petey Sarron in 1937. He followed this up a year later with a points victory over reigning welterweight holder Barney Ross, and achieved his hat-trick of world titles when he claimed the lightweight crown following a split decision over Lou Ambers in August 1938.

Armstrong had fought an amazing 180 bouts by the time he retired in 1945 and his record proudly stood at 149 wins (KO 101), 21 defeats (KO 2) and 10 draws. Sadly, Armstrong later spiralled into a drugs and alcohol-fuelled nightmare and was blind and penniless by the time he died in October 1988.

Baer

Max Baer's career could have realised its true potential had he the commitment to train in preparation for his fights. Although the crowd loved his inability to take his fights seriously – he would often clown about in the ring – the "Livermore Larruper" could, and should, have had a far more glittering record.

As it was, Baer – born Maximilian Adelbert Baer on 11 February 1909 in Moaha, Nebraska – won just one world championship bout. That was against Primo Carnera on 14 June 1934 when Baer demolished the Italian, putting his opponent (who was 50 pounds heavier) on the canvas a staggering 11 times in 11 rounds before the fight was halted, to grab the heavyweight belt.

Baer had turned professional in 1929 and went into his title fight with 39 victories and seven defeats to his name.

▲ Max Baer brought the thrill back into boxing.

His first attempted defence did not go according to plan and he found himself on the wrong end of a shock unanimous decision against James J Braddock the following year. He continued fighting but never got another shot at the title, and retired in 1941 with a record of 68 wins (KO 52) 13 defeats (KO 3). He carved out a second career as a radio personality but died in November 1959 at the age of 50.

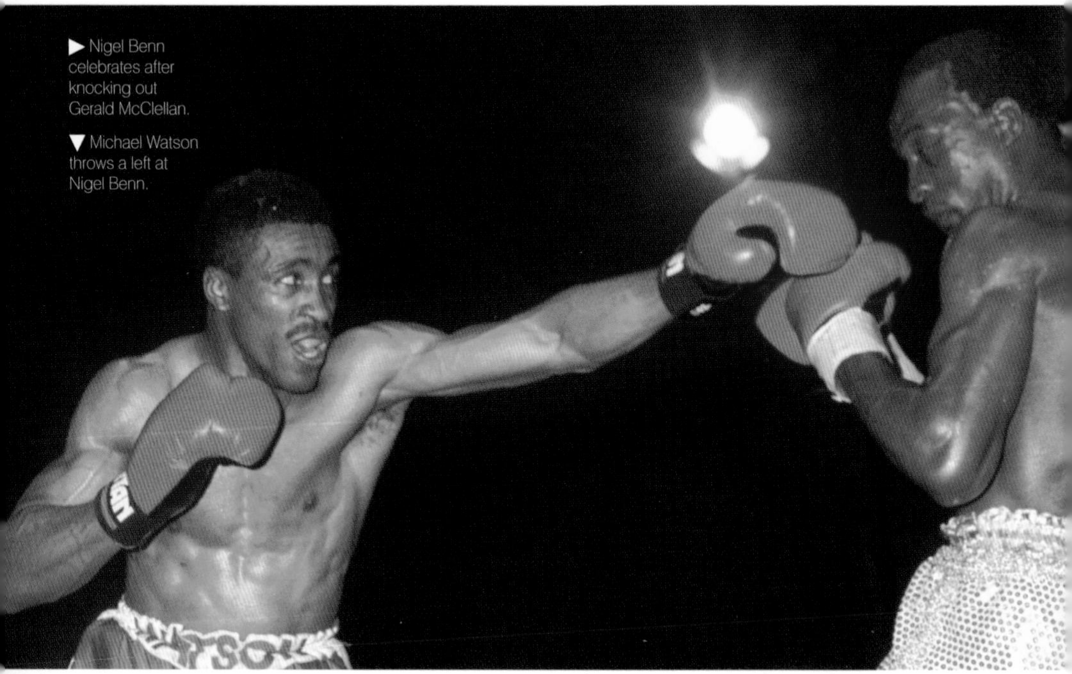

▶ Nigel Benn celebrates after knocking out Gerald McClellan.

▼ Michael Watson throws a left at Nigel Benn.

Benn

British boxers were a dominant force in the super middleweight division during the 1990s and, along with archrival Chris "Simply the Best" Eubank, Nigel the "Dark Destroyer" Benn grabbed many of the headlines.

Benn – born in Ilford on 22 January 1964 and the cousin of former England footballer Paul Ince – turned professional in 1987 and embarked on a 22-fight unbeaten streak that was ended by Michael Watson in May 1989 with a sixth round knockout. Within a year, however, Benn had been crowned WBO middleweight champion with an eight round stoppage of Doug DeWitt. He successfully defended this title just once before losing to Eubank in November 1990.

Benn soon stepped up to super middleweight and contested the WBC belt with Mauro Galvano. Such was Benn's ferocity that the fight was stopped in the fourth round with the champion badly cut. Benn embarked on a series of title defences that included a battering draw with Eubank, who had put his own WBO belt up for grabs, and a disastrous night that saw Gerald McClellan seriously injured before losing to Thulani Malinga in March 1996. Two more fights followed that year against WBO champion Steve Collins but the Irishman was too strong and recorded fourth and sixth round knockouts. Benn retired to become a DJ but found religion and is now an ordained minister in Tenerife.

Berg

▶ The awesome Jack Berg.

▶▶ Jack Berg in training.

There can be few fighters who could claim to have fought over 70 professional fights before reaching the grand old age of 20 – it's no wonder that Jack Berg earned the nickname "Kid". Born Judah Bergman in London on 28 June 1909, Berg hung up his amateur gloves aged just 14 and was soon standing toe to toe with some of the biggest names in the ring such as Johnny Cuthbert, Harry Corbett and Billy Petrolle.

Berg was nicknamed the "Whitechapel Windmill" because his arms never stopped moving during each three-minute round. His moment of glory came in February 1930 when he stripped Mushy Callahan of his light welterweight title with a 10th round stoppage. Berg's previous fight had been against Tony Canzoneri but the American had won what many were already calling the Fight of the Decade by a split decision. The pair would line up against each other on two further occasions for the world lightweight title but Berg could not find a way to claim a second belt.

He was easily beaten in the third round but managed to go the distance in the return bout.

Berg served in the RAF during the Second World War and retired from the ring in 1945 after 192 fights (157 wins). He worked as a film stuntman and opened a restaurant in London before moving to Brighton. He died in April 1991.

Bowe

Riddick Bowe was something of an enigma to many critics and fans. He undoubtedly possessed a great talent but his determination and durability were constantly questioned. No-one, however, could argue with the way he dismantled undisputed heavyweight champion Evander Holyfield in November 1992. Holyfield had won his title from James

"Buster" Douglas and both men came into the fight with an undefeated record. Bowe – born in New York on 10 August 1967 – was forced to go the distance for only the fourth time in his professional career and won a unanimous decision after 12 rounds.

Bowe then courted controversy when he refused to fight the WBC

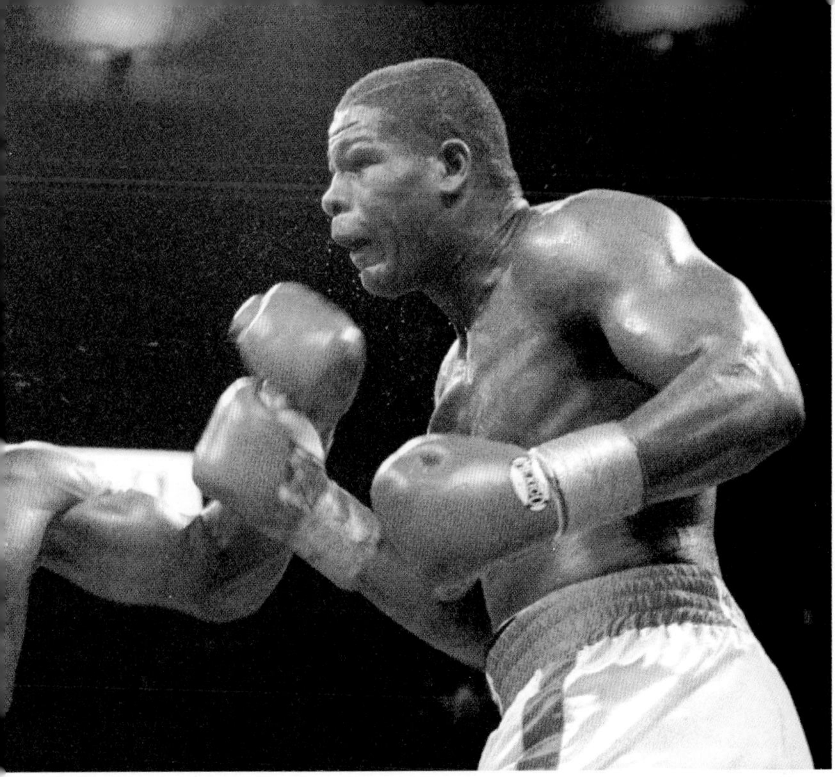

◀ Evander Holyfield (left) trades blows with his opponent Riddick Bowe during their 1992 fight.

◀◀ Riddick Bowe raises his arm in victory after winning against Herbie Hide in 1995.

number one challenger, Lennox Lewis, so relinquished that belt but then went on to stop Michael Dokes in the first round of their fight. It did not last and a rematch with Holyfield saw Bowe deposed as world champion in a fight that saw a parachutist descend into the ring and disrupt proceedings for 21 minutes. This proved to be Bowe's only defeat of his professional career and he went on to claim a further WBO title with victory over Herbie Hide in 1995. A third bout against Holyfield saw Bowe exact revenge before his life took a turn for the worse when he was imprisoned for kidnapping his wife and children. He returned to the ring in 2004 but was declared bankrupt the following year.

Bruno

▶ Frank Bruno poses with the WBC belt.

▼ Frank Bruno and Mike Tyson trade punches.

One of boxing's most popular characters, Franklin Roy Bruno – born in London on 16 November 1961 – seemed to be the perennial underachiever as he lost his first three title fights. The first, against Tim Witherspoon, ended in the 11th round of their 1986 WBA heavyweight title contest.

The second saw heavyweight legend Mike Tyson stop Bruno in the fifth round in 1989. The result was not really a surprise to anyone as Tyson was much quicker than the lumbering Bruno, who had hit the canvas as early as the first round. Bruno's third opportunity came against WBC champion Lennox Lewis in 1993 but there was a similar story as the fight was stopped in the seventh round. Big Frank did, however, get his

hands on the WBC belt in 1995 when he outpointed Oliver McCall. Sadly, his reign ended in the next bout with Tyson stopping him in the third round of a fight that proved to be Bruno's last.

Bruno finished with a career record of 40 wins (KO 38) and five defeats (all by knockout). The only times he had to rely on the judges for a decision were in November 1984 against Philip Brown and his title fight with McCall. Bruno became a popular pantomime regular but suffered turmoil in his personal life, being sectioned under the Mental Health Act in 2003, and admitting cocaine use two years later.

▼ Frank Bruno celebrates with the belt after his victory over Oliver McCall.

Burns

Hardly a giant in the ring in terms of stature at 5' 7" tall, Tommy Burns more than made up for his lack of height with grit, determination and boxing prowess. Born Noah Brusso in Ontario on 17

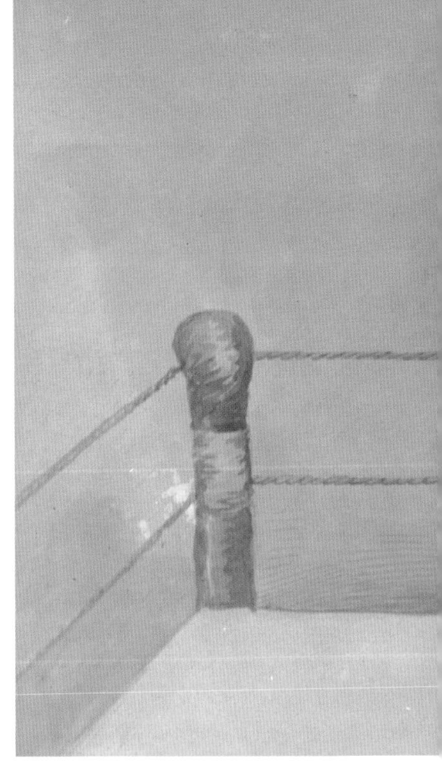

June 1881, the French-Canadian turned professional as the 20th century dawned and went on to record 43 wins (KO 34), five defeats (KO 1) and nine draws in his 58 matches.

Assuming an "Irish" name in 1904, Burns was given the chance to contest the heavyweight title two years later against Marvin Hart. Despite being

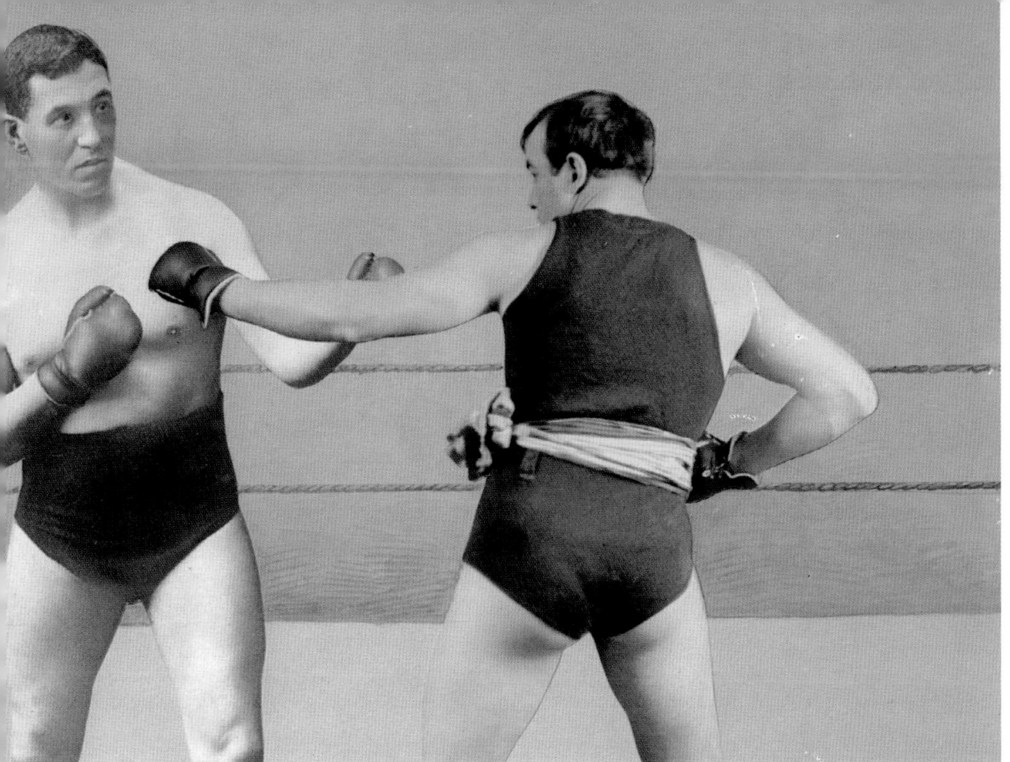

the underdog, Burns outpointed the champion over the 20 rounds and went on to successfully defend his crown 11 times over the next two years before being outfought by Jack Johnson. Burns went down in history as the first fighter to agree to contest a heavyweight title with a black boxer and it was the "Galveston Giant" who emerged victorious from their December 1908 clash in Sydney, Australia.

Burns, a shrewd businessman, never again had a shot at the world title and retired a wealthy man in 1920. He became a preacher in 1948 but died seven years later in Vancouver and was buried in a pauper's grave until a memorial plaque was erected in 1961.

▲ Tommy Burns and Jem Roche slug it out in the ring.

◀ Tommy Burns (second from right), the first boxer to hold both world heavyweight and light heavyweight titles simultaneously.

Calzaghe

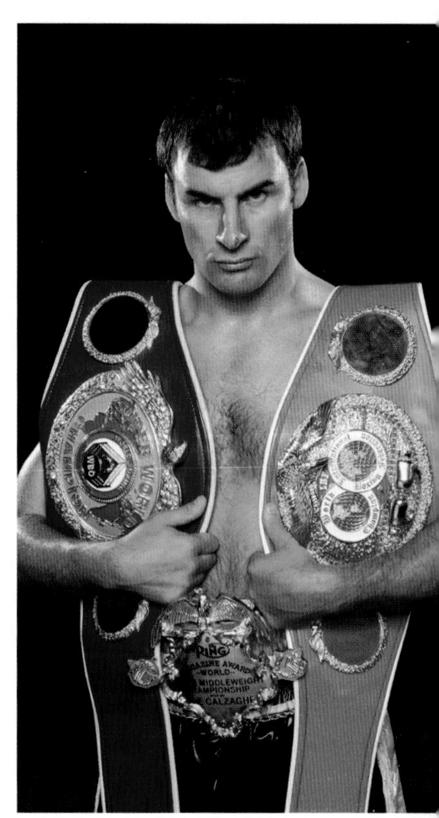

Nicknamed the "Pride of Wales", Joe Calzaghe was born in London on 23 February 1972 to an Italian father and Welsh mother. Currently living in Newport, Calzaghe is also sometimes referred to as the "Italian Dragon" due to his mixed heritage.

Calzaghe had a glittering amateur career before turning professional in 1993 and stopped seven out of his first nine opponents in the first round. The other two only managed to last until the second! He got his chance for world glory when he was picked to fight former champion Chris Eubank for the vacant WBO super middleweight title in October 1997 and grabbed it with both hands. In a thrilling spectacle, the underdog won a unanimous verdict after 12 rounds and is still undefeated, having successfully defended his title more than 20 times against the likes of

Robin Reid and Jeff Lacy. Calzaghe won a split decision victory over former middleweight and light heavyweight holder Bernard Hopkins in April 2008 in his first Stateside fight and was the unanimous victor against Ray Jones Jr later the same year. Calzaghe scored a surprise victory in the 2007 BBC Sports Personality of the Year contest when he nudged racing driver Lewis Hamilton into second place and fellow boxer Ricky Hatton into third, making him the first Welshman to win the trophy for almost 50 years.

▲ Joe Calzaghe knocks down Chris Eubank during the WBO super middleweight title fight, 1997.

◀ Joe Calzaghe with his belts.

Carpentier

▶ Georges Carpentier performing at the Alhambra, London in 1929.

▼ Georges Carpentier who was European champion at four weights.

One of the few Frenchmen to have made their mark on world boxing, Georges Carpentier was born in Lens on 12 January 1894. He was crowned the "Pride of Paris" during the height of his career and found himself treated like a movie star. This was very alien in comparison to his humble beginnings as the son of a miner but Carpentier – also nicknamed the "Orchid Man" – found fame and fortune after turning professional at the age of 14.

Carpentier fought in the French Air Force during the First World War and was awarded the *Croix de Guerre* and *Médaille Militaire* for his heroics before a return to the ring brought a world light heavyweight title bout with Battling Levinsky. The Frenchman scored such an emphatic victory over the American (in the fourth round) that he earned the opportunity for a shot at the heavyweight crown, held by the legendary Jack Dempsey.

In the first boxing match to be broadcast on radio as well as the first to take a million dollars in gate receipts, Carpentier was unlucky to break his right hand in the second round and despite his efforts the fight was stopped in the fourth with Dempsey unmarked. The two remained close friends until Carpentier's death in October 1975.

▲ Marcel Cerdan delivers a hard right to Tony Zale.

Cerdan

Marcel Cerdan became France's biggest boxing hero, following in the footsteps of Georges Carpentier, and it was a tragedy that he was cut down in his prime when the plane he and his manager had been travelling in crashed into a mountain in the Azores on 27 October 1949. Such was the feeling of loss that France declared a national day of mourning.

Marcellin Cerdan – born on 22 July 1916 in French Algeria – had turned professional in 1934 and was fast becoming a name to be taken seriously with 45 straight victories before disqualification in the fifth round of his match against Harry Craster ended his winning streak in January 1939. Undeterred, Cerdan claimed the world middleweight crown in September 1948, when Tony Zale retired in the 12th round of their contest at the Roosevelt Stadium in New Jersey.

Cerdan's first title defence was against Jake LaMotta, and the

▲ Marcel Cerdan and Jake LaMotta exchange blows.

Frenchman was floored in the first round by a mighty left hook. In hitting the canvas, Cerdan suffered an injury that forced him to retire in the 10th round, but a rematch was set up and tickets were selling fast as punters were eager to see this Frenchman who had only lost four times in 115 fights. Little did they know that he had already fought his last battle.

Charles

▲ Ezzard Charles (left) in action against Jersey Joe Walcott during their world heavyweight title fight in Chicago, 1949.

Rated the greatest light heavyweight of all by *Ring* magazine, Ezzard Charles never won a world title in that division. He did, however, claim the world heavyweight crown and proudly wore the belt between 1949 and 1951.

Charles, born on 27 July 1921 in Georgia, was nicknamed the "Cincinnati Cobra" and turned professional in 1940. He received his break when Joe Louis retired in 1949 and Charles was chosen to face "Jersey" Joe Walcott to contest the vacant title. The fight took place on 22 June in Chicago and Charles won a unanimous decision after 15 rounds. He successfully defended his title against Gus Lesnevich, Pat Valentino and Freddie Beshore before agreeing to fight former champion Louis, who had returned to the ring because of financial difficulties. Charles emerged the victor on points but suffered mixed emotions because Louis had been his hero.

Walcott would prove to be a regular adversary and Charles stopped him in the seventh round of their rematch. Unfortunately, in their two other clashes, Walcott out-boxed his opponent to claim and then retain the title. Charles twice fought for the world crown again, both matches ending in defeat against Rocky Marciano in 1954, but financial problems delayed his retirement and he lost 17 of his last 29 bouts. He died in May 1975 and was elected to the International Boxing Hall of Fame in 1990.

▼ Julio Cesar Chavez celebrates after defeating Roger Mayweather

Chavez

Rated by the majority of critics and fans alike as the greatest pound for pound boxer of the 20th century, Julio Cesar Chavez defied time and was still boxing professionally when he was 43 years old. He eventually retired in 2005 with a record of 107 wins (KO 86) six defeats (KO 4) and two draws with four of those losses coming during his last 11 fights. Indeed, such was his talent and determination that Chavez suffered his first reversal against Frankie Randall in 1994, an incredible 14 years and 90 fights after he turned professional.

The fame and fortune that he earned was so different to Chavez's childhood in Mexico. Born Julio Cesar Chavez Gonzalez on 12 July 1962, "JC" – as he was affectionately known – grew up in an abandoned railway carriage with his five sisters and four brothers (three of whom also became professional boxers).

He first put on boxing gloves at the age of 16 and turned professional two years later. Chavez claimed six world titles in three divisions during his career and is probably best remembered for his battles with Roger Mayweather,

Meldrick Taylor and Oscar De La Hoya as well as the records he holds for most successful title defences (27) and most title fights (37).

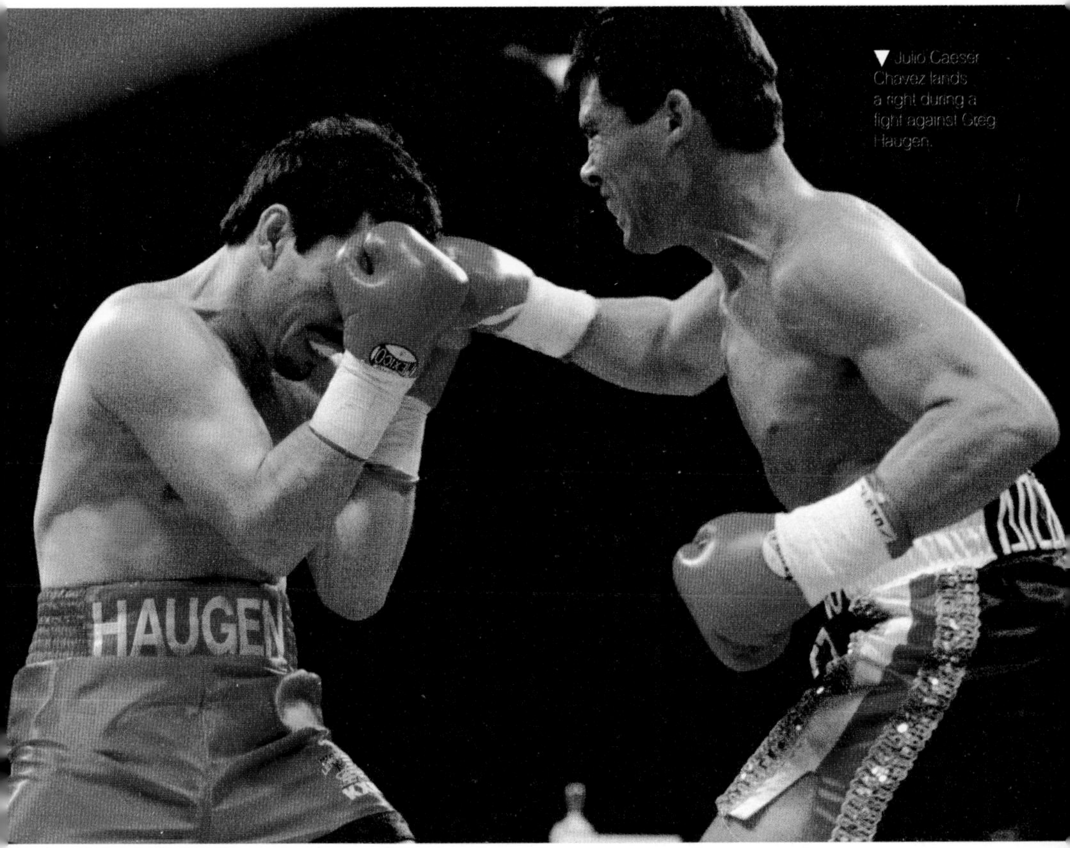

▼ Julio Caeser Chavez lands a right during a fight against Greg Haugen.

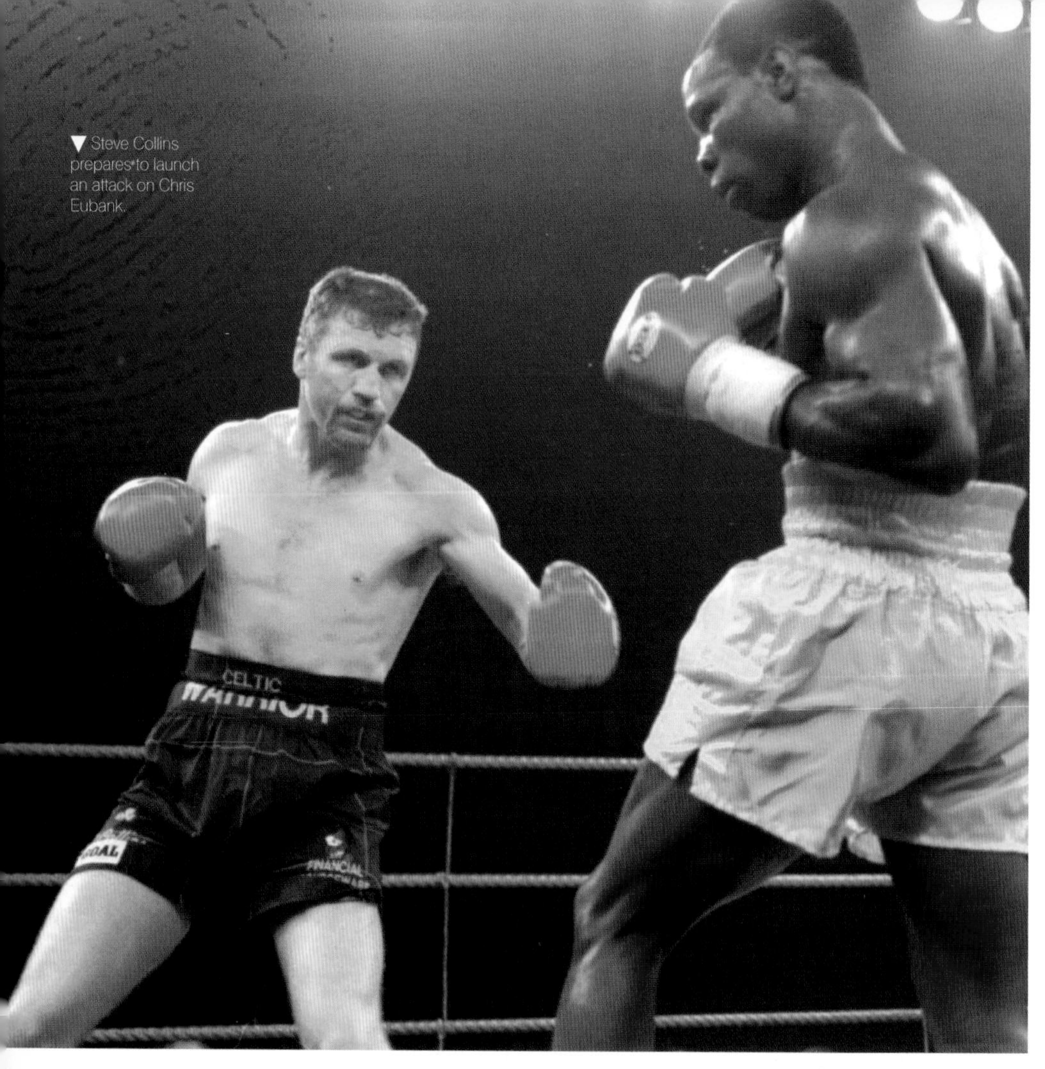

▼ Steve Collins prepares to launch an attack on Chris Eubank.

Collins

Steve Collins (aka the "Celtic Warrior") may have only fought 39 times during his professional career but he can claim never to have been stopped in a match. He won 36 of his bouts (21 KO) and the only losses he suffered after turning professional in 1986 were when he went the distance with Mike McCallum, Reggie Johnson and Sumbu Kalambay.

These three fights were all for middleweight belts, but Collins, born in Dublin on 21 July 1964, did get his hands on the WBO crown when he stopped Chris Pyatt in the fifth round of their world title fight in Sheffield in May 1994. Collins did not defend this title, however, as he stepped up to super middleweight to replace Ray Close, who had to pull out of a match with holder Chris Eubank in March 1995.

The clash was one of *the* fights of the decade, as was the rematch six months later, and the Irishman came out on top in both contests. He went on to successfully defend his WBO title on another six occasions – including two against the other great super middleweight of the era, Nigel Benn – before retiring. It was rumoured that Collins would make a comeback to fight Joe Calzaghe and Roy Jones Jr but made his retirement permanent on medical advice after collapsing during sparring.

▼ Steve Collins holds aloft his WBO super middleweight belt after defeating Craig Cummings.

Cooper

▶ Muhammad Ali and Henry Cooper shake hands after Ali's victory.

▶▶ Henry Cooper wearing his three Lonsdale belts.

Undoubtedly one of the nation's favourite boxers, "Our 'Enery" found his tendency to cut more easily than his opponents to be the biggest obstacle to his ambition of becoming a world champion. Born a twin on 3 May 1934 in London, Henry Cooper is the only British boxer ever to have held three Lonsdale Belts.

Cooper's career is best remembered for the two clashes he fought with Muhammad Ali. The first, in 1963, was a non-title meeting against the then Cassius Clay. The Englishman had the American on the canvas in the fourth round but the fight was stopped in the fifth with Cooper suffering from a badly cut face. The rematch – Cooper's only shot at a world title – three years later saw a similar result, with the referee stopping the fight in the sixth round.

Cooper went on to fight such notable boxers as Floyd Patterson and Joe Bugner before retiring in March 1971 with a record of 40 victories (KO 27), 14 defeats (KO 8) and one draw in his 55 bouts. He went on to be a television personality through the quiz show *A Question Of Sport* and adverts for Brut aftershave before becoming the first boxer to be honoured with a knighthood in 2000.

C

Corbett

▶ A poster promoting the 1892 "Grand Glove Contest" between John L Sullivan and James J Corbett.

Life as a boxer in the sport's early days was certainly not dull. James Corbett – known as "Gentleman Jim" – turned professional in 1884 but his fight against Peter Jackson in May 1891 turned into a marathon. The two were fighting for a purse of $10,000, with $1,500 going to the loser, but the bout became tame after 30 rounds, with the two circling each other in the ring and very few, if any, blows landing. The bout started at 9.28pm and ended at 1.33am when it was declared a no contest.

Corbett, born on 1 September 1866 in San Francisco, did write his name in the history books, however, when he defeated heavyweight champion John L Sullivan in the first title fight held under the new Marquess of Queensberry Rules in September 1892 with a knockout in round 21.

He defended his crown against Charley Mitchell two years later but then had to wait until 1897 before his next title fight; that was against Bob Fitzsimmons and Corbett was stopped

C

in round 14. He went on to contest two more title fights (both against James J Jeffries) before retiring in 1903. Credited with bringing more skill and thought into the art of boxing, Corbett died in February 1933.

De La Hoya

▶ Oscar De La Hoya in celebratory mood after beating Jimmy Bredahl.

▶▶ Oscar De La Hoya (left) throws a left hook against Ricardo Mayorga (right) during the WBC light middleweight title fight in 2006.

The fights that Oscar "Golden Boy" De La Hoya has contested throughout his career have generated more than $500 million, making him the richest boxer ever. To his credit, De La Hoya has always wanted to pit himself against the best opponents available rather than taking on second-rate fighters merely to cash in on his world titles.

De La Hoya, born in Los Angeles on 4 February 1973, turned professional in 1992 and won the WBO super featherweight title in only his 12th bout, knocking out Jimmy Bredahl in the 10th round of their March 1994 contest. He went on to add lightweight, light welterweight and welterweight titles to his portfolio before suffering his first defeat against Felix Trinidad in 1999. Since then, De La Hoya has also claimed light middleweight belts.

Shane Mosley has been a thorn in his side, with two defeats, while De La Hoya failed in his bid to claim Bernard Hopkins' middleweight crown when "The Executioner" inflicted the only knockout of his career so far. De La Hoya successfully fought Ricardo Mayorga for his WBC light middleweight belt in 2006 but lost his first defence against Floyd Mayweather Jr. He returned to winning ways against Steve Forbes in May 2008.

Dempsey

When Jack Dempsey announced his retirement in January 1928, boxing lost one of its first superstars. Many of his fights had set new financial and attendance records but he was having trouble with his left eye muscle. Three months later, he declared he would not make a comeback – not even for $50 million. He told the press that he had made enough money and his health was still good, stating, "I can still walk around and tell the time." It turned out to be a wise decision because the "Manassa Mauler" – born William Harrison Dempsey on 24 June 1893 in Colorado – went on to live to the ripe old age of 87.

Dempsey had turned professional in 1914 and claimed the world heavyweight title with a third round knockout of Jess Willard in July 1919. He successfully defended his title on five occasions before losing to Gene Tunney on points in September 1926. His last fight was a rematch with Tunney that had the same outcome, after which Dempsey announced his retirement. The only time he suffered a knockout was against Fireman Jim Flynn in 1917 and his career record reads 66 wins (KO 51) six defeats (KO 1) and 11 draws.

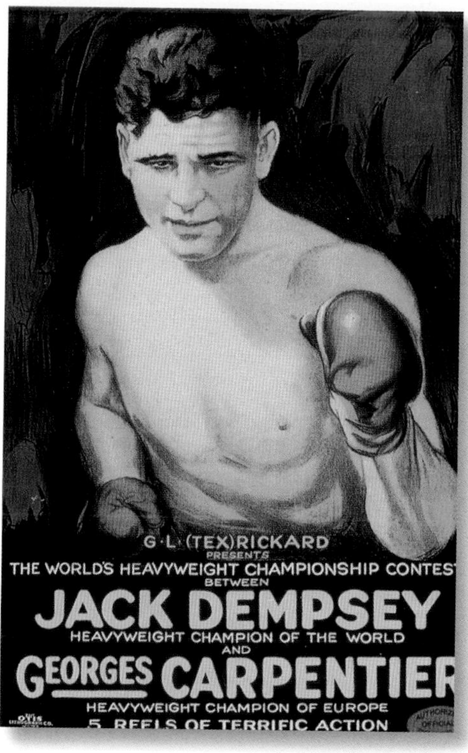

◀ A poster promoting the 1921 match between Jack Dempsey and Georges Carpentier.

◀◀ Jack Dempsey before his 1926 fight against Gene Tunney.

▶ Jim Driscoll who was the first featherweight to win a Lonsdale belt.

▶▶ Italian born American boxer Johnny Dundee with (from left), Welsh boxer Jim Driscoll, Ted "Kid" Lewis and the man who had managed them all, 1924.

Driscoll

Remembered for being the "uncrowned champion of the world" and "peerless", Jim Driscoll was born in Cardiff on 15 December 1880 and was one of the most skilful boxers of his era. Sadly, he did not possess the punching power to cement his dominance in many fights as demonstrated in one notorious bout against world featherweight champion Abe Attell in New York in February 1909.

Difficult as it may be to comprehend today, New York was then governed by Frawley Law which allowed boxing matches to take place but only if there was no decision at the end. It meant, therefore, that the only way a fight could be decided was by knockout and many world champions took advantage of this loophole and only agreed to fight in this city.

The papers unanimously gave their verdict to Driscoll but, as Attell was still on his feet at the end of 10 rounds, Driscoll returned to Wales empty handed.

Driscoll never contested an official world title bout but did win British and

European titles before retiring in 1919 – military service had halted his career and he only fought three times after the First World War – with a record of 63 wins (KO 39) four defeats (KO 1) and six draws. He did not have long to enjoy his retirement, however, as he died on 30 January 1925 of pneumonia.

Duran

▼ One of the few bouts that Duran lost, this time against Robbie Sims.

One of the greatest boxers of all time, Roberto Duran is the only one to have fought in five different decades. Duran, born on 16 June 1951 in Panama, turned professional in 1967 and fought his last bout in July 2001 against Hector Camacho.

The intervening years showed why "Manos de Piedra" (Hands of Stone) was able to continue for so long in such a brutal sport. He won his first belt, the WBA lightweight title, by seeing off Ken Buchanan in June 1972 and went on to add further world crowns at welterweight, junior middleweight and middleweight before the end of the 1980s.

One of the highlights of his career was when he stepped up to welterweight to take on the great "Sugar" Ray Leonard in June 1980. Duran fought a tactical bout that did not allow Leonard time or space and won a shock points decision. Leonard won the rematch five months later when Duran dramatically quit in the eighth round.

Duran rebuilt his reputation and went on to fight such legends as Wilfred Benitez, Marvin Hagler, Thomas Hearns and Iran Barkley in a career that saw him win 103 times (KO 70) and lose on 16 (KO 4) occasions.

▲ Roberto Duran trades punches with Sugar Ray Leonard during their 1989 fight.

Eubank

▶ Chris Eubank at the end of the ninth round after beating Nigel Benn.

▶▶ Chris Eubank (left) and Michael Watson (right) square up during the WBO middleweight title fight, June 1991.

You either loved Chris Eubank for his brash, arrogant swagger… or you hated him for his brash, arrogant swagger! What no one can deny, however, is his talent in the ring and his refusal to admit defeat.

Born in London on 8 August 1966, Christopher Livingstone Eubanks spent his very early life in Jamaica before returning to England. Being labelled as a problem child for trying to protect children from bullies, as well as being expelled from school and shunted around various institutions, gave Eubank the determination to succeed. He moved to New York to live with his mother in 1982 and started training, turning professional three years later.

His first shot at a world title came in November 1990 when he took on WBO middleweight champion Nigel Benn in a bruising encounter that

was stopped in the ninth round. His final defence of this title came against Michael Watson in June 1991 and the pair lined up for the vacant WBO middleweight belt three months later in a fight that was to have a dramatic impact on their lives. Both men collapsed exhausted at the end of the bout but, while Eubank recovered, Watson spent 40 days in a coma and was left disabled. While Eubank made a successful return to the ring, many feel he had lost some of his killer instinct following the Watson fight.

Eubank went on to make 14

successful defences of his title that included classic encounters with Nigel Benn (again), Ray Close and Graciano Rocchigiani (where he enraged the crowd by strutting and posing between rounds). Indeed, he was supposed to be having a rematch with Close in 1995 but his opponent failed a brain scan and Irishman Steve Collins was lined up as a replacement. As it turned out, Eubank was unable to finish off a bloody Collins and lost both his title and his unbeaten record to a unanimous decision, although the rematch was closer with the judges being split in the Irishman's favour.

Eubank announced his retirement but returned to the ring the following year before lining up with Joe Calzaghe for the vacant WBO super middleweight title in 1997. Again, Eubank lost on points but stepped up to take on WBO cruiserweight holder Carl Thompson in 1998. The judges awarded Thompson a points decision in the first fight and the referee stopped the rematch in the 10th round despite Eubank's protests. This proved to be his final contest but the ever-eccentric Eubank would still hit the headlines with regularity.

Fitzsimmons

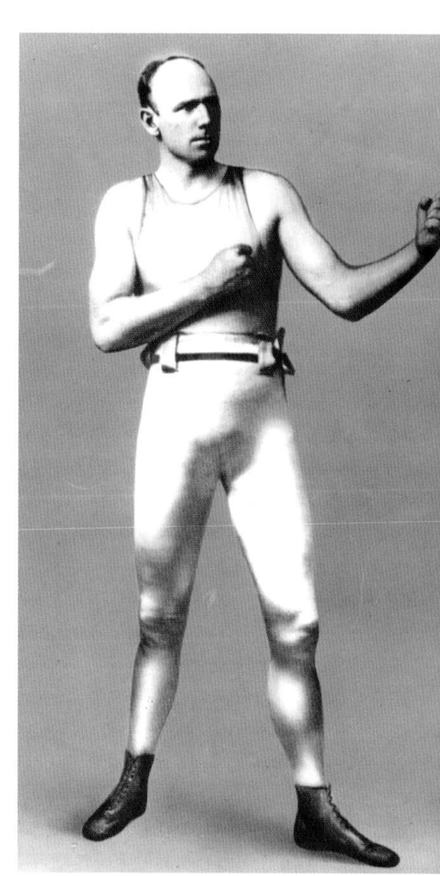

Born in Helston, Cornwall, on 26 May 1863, Robert James Fitzsimmons' life has many similarities to Lennox Lewis'. Although born in England, the Fitzsimmons family emigrated to New Zealand when Bob was a youngster. There he became a blacksmith, building the upper body muscles that would serve him so well in the ring. Fitzsimmons went on to become England's first undisputed heavyweight champion of the world...a record he held until Lewis – born in London, brought up in Canada – beat Evander Holyfield in 1999.

Fitzsimmons turned professional in the 1880s – his first recorded bout was against Joe Riddell in 1885 – and became the first boxer to win world titles in three divisions; middleweight against Jack Dempsey (1891), heavyweight against James J Corbett (1897) and light

◀ Bob Fitzsimmons supplemented his boxing earnings by acting.

◀◀ Bob Fitzsimmons, the first boxer to win three championship divisions.

heavyweight against George Gardiner (1903). Dempsey had been on the canvas so many times that Fitzsimmons begged him to throw in the towel but the champion refused. With no alternative, Fitzsimmons promptly knocked out his opponent and carried him to his corner.

Nicknamed "Ruby", Fitzsimmons retired in 1914 having won 50 (KO 44), lost eight (KO 7) and drawn five of his fights. He died of pneumonia in Chicago in October 1917.

Foreman

Like so many others who turned to boxing as a vocation, George Foreman was born into poverty on 22 January 1948 in Marshall, Texas. He lived with his mother and stepfather and could very well have ended up in prison had he not discovered boxing instead of turning to crime, like many of his peers.

His first major achievement in the ring was winning the heavyweight gold medal at the 1968 Olympic Games in Mexico City and he turned professional the following year. He soon built up a reputation as a fighter to be feared and won 37 consecutive bouts before lining up against WBC and WBA holder Joe Frazier. The champion was expected to make mincemeat of Foreman on his way to a rematch with Muhammad Ali but Foreman, not for the last time, upset the form book with a tremendous display of boxing. He had Frazier on the canvas three times in the first round and another three times in the second round before the fight was stopped by the referee.

Two successful defences followed, against Joe Roman (a first round knockout) and Ken Norton (he lasted just two rounds), the man who had previously broken Ali's jaw, before an eagerly anticipated clash with Ali himself. Dubbed the "Rumble in the Jungle", the fight took place in Zaire in October 1974 and surpassed all expectations in terms of entertainment. For the first seven rounds, the challenger allowed himself to be pummelled on the ropes before unleashing an attack on Foreman that saw the champion hit the deck in the eighth round. Ali summed it up as his "rope a dope" strategy while Foreman promptly retired.

His retirement did not last long, however, as he made a comeback in January 1976 in an attempt to make some money after he had blown his previous earnings. Things were going well with victories over Ron Lyle and Joe Frazier but a 1977 defeat to Jimmy Young prompted a second retirement as Foreman became a preacher.

This would last for 10 years but he again returned to the ring and later took on WBC, WBA and IBF champion Evander Holyfield in April 1991. This ended in a unanimous decision for the holder, as did the clash with Tommy Morrison for the vacant WBO heavyweight title in June 1993, but Foreman became the oldest man ever to win a heavyweight title when he defeated WBA and IBF holder Michael Moorer in November 1995. Foreman's last fight was a defeat to Shannon Briggs in November 1997 and he is now just as famous for his pioneering Lean Mean Grilling Machine as for his exploits in the ring.

◀ George Foreman after winning gold at the 1968 Mexico Olympics.

▼ George Foreman with his IBF and WBA belts.

Frazier

▶ Joe Frazier and Joe Bugner during a world title eliminator fight.

▼ Joe Frazier on his way to victory at the 1964 Olympics.

"Smokin" Joe Frazier is best remembered for his trilogy of clashes with Muhammad Ali but he also fought other notable boxers such as Joe Bugner and George Foreman.

Joseph William Frazier was born in South Carolina on 12 January 1944 and claimed the heavyweight gold at the 1964 Olympics in Tokyo before turning professional a year later. Within three years, the world title would be his, although it was not recognised by everybody. After Ali had been stripped of his title for refusing the Draft, rival boxing organisations set up their own competitions to determine the world champion. Frazier beat Buster Mathis to claim the NYSAC world heavyweight crown and added the WBC and WBA belts when he stopped Jimmy Ellis in the fifth round two years later to become undisputed champion.

Frazier was expected to lose to former champion Ali in 1971 but obviously did not read the script, winning on points. His next notable fight saw him paired with George Foreman and, two rounds into the bout, Frazier was no longer champion of the world. He suffered two more defeats, by Ali (1974 and 1975) and another at the hands of Foreman (1976), before calling time on his career. He was drawn out of retirement for one match with Floyd Cummings in 1981 that ended in a draw but returned to training youngsters at his gym in Philadelphia.

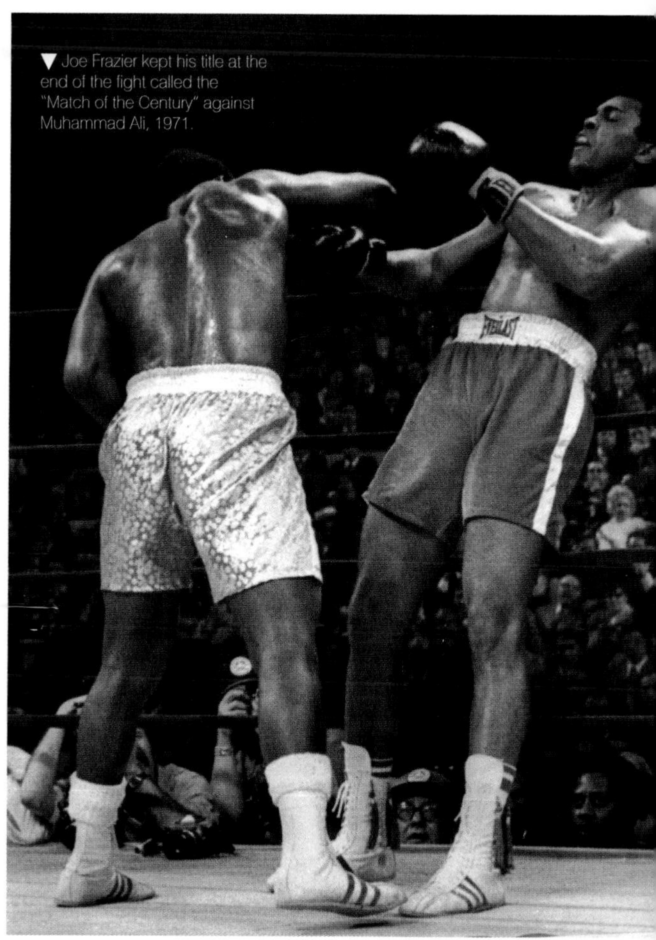

▼ Joe Frazier kept his title at the end of the fight called the "Match of the Century" against Muhammad Ali, 1971.

Graziano

He may have only won one world championship bout and lost three, but Rocky Graziano will forever be remembered by boxing fans everywhere for his courage and skill in the ring. Born on 1 January 1922 in New York, Thomas Rocco Barbella fell into a life of petty crime before being called up to the US Army. He wasn't one to take orders, however, and ended up in the military prison before being dishonourably discharged.

Having changed his name in an attempt at a fresh start, Graziano turned professional in 1942 and worked his way up the ranks to win the right to challenge Tony Zale for the world middleweight title in September 1946. The champion retained his crown with a sixth round knockout, but not before both men had hit the canvas in the first. The rematch, the following year, saw a reversal in fortunes as Graziano unleashed a barrage at the champion in the sixth round which prompted the referee to halt proceedings. A third encounter between the two in 1948 saw Zale regain his title with a third round knockout.

Graziano went on to

unsuccessfully contest one more title fight, against Sugar Ray Robinson in 1952, before retiring the same year with a career record of 67 wins (KO 52), 10 defeats (KO 3) and six draws. Rocky Graziano died in May 1990.

◀ Rocky Graziano, one of the most popular fighters of his era.

◀◀ Rocky Graziano.

▶ Harry Greb.

▶▶ Harry Greb was a fast and aggressive fighter.

Greb

One of the most prolific fighters ever, Harry Greb contested 299 bouts (winning 260) during his short life. He was born Edward Henry Greb on 6 June 1894 in Pittsburgh and turned professional in 1913, quickly earning the nickname of the "Human Windmill" for his aggressive style that often saw his opponents wither under a barrage of punches.

Often fighting up to five or six times a month – something that is inconceivable to today's generation of boxers who may have one or two bouts a year – it is, perhaps, surprising that Greb didn't challenge for a world title until August 1923. Utilising a more orthodox style, in fear of being disqualified, Greb and middleweight champion Johnny Wilson boxed their way through 15 rounds of mediocrity with neither allegedly in danger of hitting the canvas. The judges gave Greb the title on points and he retained his crown for three years until losing on points to Tiger Flowers in February 1926. Greb tried to reclaim his belt in a rematch six months later but the result was the same.

That was the last time that Harry Greb graced the ring as he was run over by a car and forced into hospital for a routine operation. Unfortunately, Greb never came round from the anaesthetic and died on 22 October 1926.

Hagler

Marvin Hagler had everything that boxing fans wanted during his peak in the 1980s – grit, determination, speed and power – so it is little wonder that Americans took him into their hearts and nicknamed him "Marvelous". Born Marvin Nathaniel in Newark on 23 May 1954, Hagler was a late convert to pugilism and only turned professional at the age of 21.

He worked his way up to become number one challenger but was forced to watch as lesser rivals were given title shots against the likes of Carlos Monzon and Hugo Corro.

Hagler eventually got the opportunity to claim a world title in November 1979 when he faced WBA and WBC middleweight holder Vito Antuofermo but, in a move that bemused many spectators, the contest was declared a draw. Hagler had to wait for his chance for revenge because Antuofermo promptly lost to Alan Minter, but did get his hands on the belts when he stopped the Briton in the third round in 1980. Hagler went on to successfully defend his title on 12

◀ A bout between Marvin Hagler and Sugar Ray Leonard, 1987.

◀◀ A triumphant Marvin Hagler after his fight with Alan Minter was stopped in the third round.

occasions over the next six years. His last fight was against "Sugar" Ray Leonard in 1987, a fight Hagler was so sure he had won – though it was awarded to Leonard on a split decision – that he never fought again.

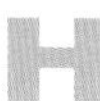

Hamed

While it is less irritating to be cocky and arrogant when fights are being won convincingly and entertainingly, "Prince" Naseem Hamed found that many spectators deserted him once he lost his air of invincibility. Born to Yemeni parents in Sheffield on 12 February 1974, Hamed was just what boxing needed in wthe mid to late 1990s. Many superstars of the previous era had faded or retired and the arrival of the cocksure Yorkshire lad breathed fresh air into the sport.

Hamed turned professional in 1992 and within three years and 20 fights was world champion after dethroning WBO featherweight king Steve Robinson in the fifth round. Hamed began defending his belt and quickly added the WBC title to his name. Famed for his elaborate entrances as much as his boxing skills, fans tuned in to watch him demolish his opponents – usually within the first few rounds – but he suffered his first and only defeat in April 2001. Competing against Marco Antonio Barrera for the vacant IBO featherweight crown, Hamed found the unanimous verdict going against him.

His confidence apparently dented, Hamed did return the following year to beat Manuel Calvo but has not fought since despite frequent rumours to the contrary. A custodial sentence in May 2006 for dangerous driving certainly seemed to signal the end of an entertaining career.

◀ Prince Naseem Hamed stands over Steve Robinson after winning the WBO featherweight championship of the world, 1995.

◀◀ Prince Naseem Hamed retains his WBO title by knocking down Said Lawal in the first 35 seconds, 1996.

Hatton

When Ricky Hatton fought WBC welterweight champion Floyd Mayweather Jr in December 2007, it was one of the most eagerly awaited bouts in recent years. Thousands of Hatton's fans made the journey from Manchester to Las Vegas and created an atmosphere that must have made the "Hitman" feel he was boxing at home. Unfortunately, the American ruined the party and the contest was stopped in the 10th round with Hatton suffering the first defeat of his professional career.

Richard Hatton, born on 6 October 1978 in Stockport, has been rated by many as one of the greatest British fighters of all time. He turned professional in 1997 and won the vacant WBU light welterweight title with a fourth round stoppage of Tony Pep in March 2001. Hatton added IBF, IBC and WBC light welterweight belts and stepped up to claim WBA welterweight champion Luis Collazo's crown in May 2006.

Ring magazine named Hatton their 2005 Fighter of the Year making him the first British boxer to receive the award since its inception in 1928. With a record of 44 wins (31 KO) and just the one defeat by the age of 30, Hatton recorded a unanimous decision in his May 2008 meeting with IBO light welterweight holder Juan Lazcano.

▲ Ricky Hatton celebrates after he retained his WBU title against Carlos Vilches, 2004.

◀ Luis Collazo ducks a right from Ricky Hatton during their WBA title fight.

▲ Larry Holmes and Evander Holyfield trade punches.

▶ Larry Holmes taking a breather in his match against Evander Holyfield.

Holmes

Larry the "Easton Assassin" Holmes fell just short of matching Rocky Marciano's record of going 49 fights without defeat. Marciano retired after his 49th bout but Holmes lost to Michael Spinks, thereby losing the chance to equal this feat.

Holmes – born on 3 November 1949 in Cuthbert, Georgia – was disqualified for holding in the final of the trials to select the team to represent the US at the 1972 Olympics. Disillusioned with the amateur game, he turned professional the following year and began a winning streak that astounded many, considering he was up against boxers of such calibre as Ken Norton, Tim Witherspoon, Gerry Clooney and Muhammad Ali. His first title shot came in June 1978 when he took on WBC heavyweight champion Ken Norton. A split decision after 15 rounds saw Holmes awarded the belt and he embarked on a run of 17 successful title defences before relinquishing the belt to become the champion of the newly-formed IBF. He reigned supreme until meeting light heavyweight Spinks in 1985 and lost the rematch the following year. Further attempts to regain the heavyweight championship failed against Mike Tyson (1988), Evander Holyfield (1992), Oliver McCall (1995) and Brian Nielsen (1997) before Holmes finally retired in 2002.

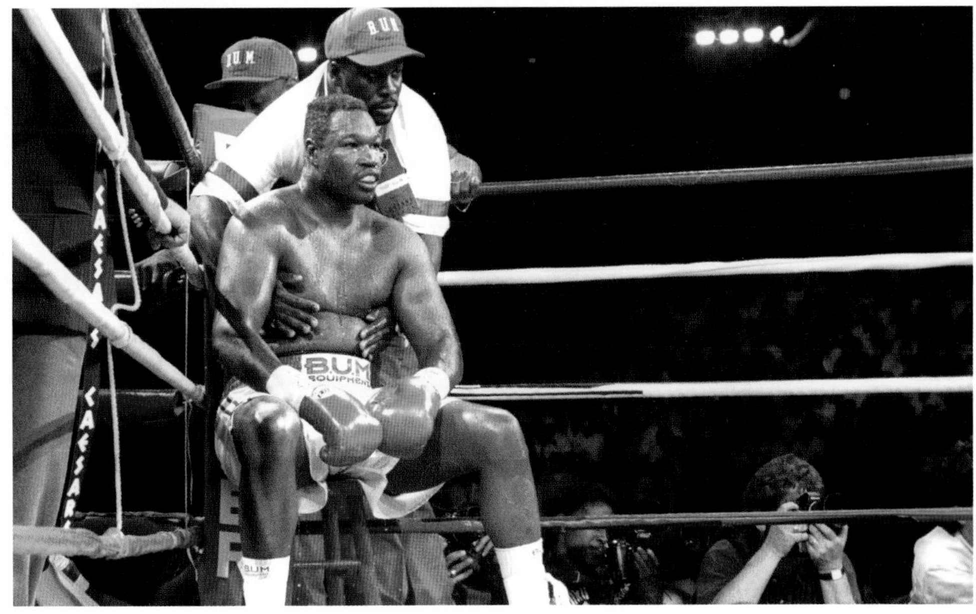

Bank of America
Coca-Cola CLASSIC
GRAND GARDEN
The One and Only Original. RCA
WARRIOR
GOLD BEER

Holyfield

Evander Holyfield has enjoyed a colourful career. Within two years and 12 fights of turning professional as a light heavyweight in 1984, he was crowned WBA cruiserweight world champion after a split decision following his bout with Dwight Muhammad Qawi.

Holyfield, born in Alabama on 19 October 1962, earned the nickname "The Real Deal" and had, by April 1989, unified the division with wins over IBF holder Ricky Parky and WBC champion Carlos De Leon. After the latter fight, Holyfield announced his intention to move up to heavyweight so that he could challenge Mike Tyson. Unfortunately, by the time he had worked his way to being the number one contender, Tyson had been dethroned by James "Buster" Douglas whom Holyfield stopped in the third round in October 1990 to become the undisputed heavyweight champion.

Holyfield defended his belts until he met his match in Riddick Bowe, who inflicted a first defeat with a unanimous decision after 12 rounds in November 1992. Holyfield exacted his revenge a year later but promptly lost to Michael Moorer. Famous fights with Tyson (where Holyfield had part of his ear bitten off) and Lennox Lewis (a controversial draw and then a disputed defeat) followed but Holyfield was still boxing as 2007 drew to a close, losing a unanimous decision against WBO heavyweight champion Sultan Ibragimov.

◀ The referee stops the fight in the third round as Evander Holyfield holds his ear after Mike Tyson had bitten it.

▼ Evander Holyfield on his way to losing against Sultan Ibragimov.

Ingle

▶ Paul Ingle celebrating after defending his belt against Junior Jones, 2000.

▶▶ Paul Ingle knocked out during the IBF featherweight championship of the world, 2000.

Paul Ingle was a promising boxer from Scarborough whose career was halted in its prime. Born on 22 June 1972, Ingle – nicknamed "Yorkshire Hunter" – was a member of the 1992 British Olympic Team before turning professional in 1994. He rapidly worked his way up through the ranks and was still undefeated by the time of his 22nd fight against reigning WBO featherweight champion Naseem Hamed in April 1999.

It looked all over for Ingle in the early part of the bout as he hit the canvas in the first and sixth rounds but he came back and in the ninth bloodied Hamed's nose badly and began to take control of proceedings. Having enjoyed a successful 10th round, when it looked as if Ingle might stop the champion, Hamed came out in the 11th and put Ingle away with a single left hand.

Later that year, Ingle took on Manuel Medina and claimed a unanimous decision to win the IBF featherweight title. He successfully defended his belt against Junior Jones but his next contest, against Mbulelo Botile in December 2000, saw tragedy hit. Having already been knocked down in the 11th round, Ingle remained motionless on the canvas for several minutes after the fight was stopped in the final bout before being removed from the ring on a stretcher. He was taken to the hospital where he underwent surgery to remove a blood clot from the brain.

Johansson

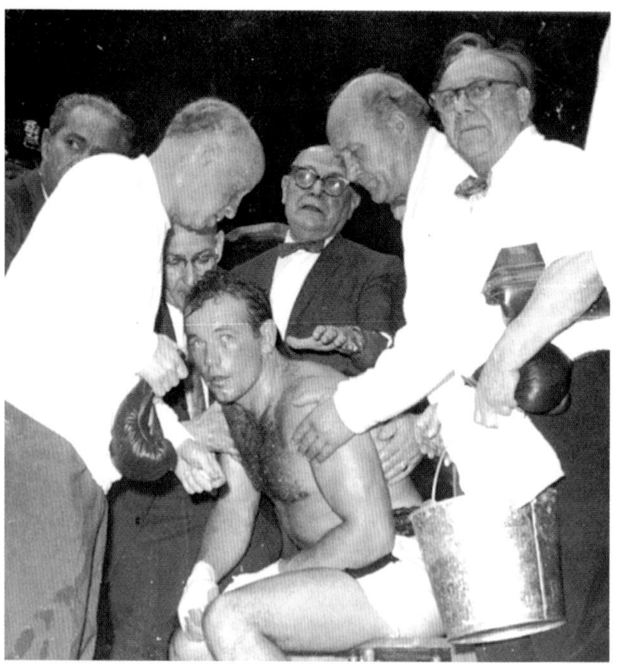

Ingemar Johansson could not have had a more inauspicious start to his boxing career. Disqualified from the heavyweight final of the 1952 Olympic Games in Helsinki for running away from his opponent and "not giving it his best", Johansson protested his innocence and claimed he was trying to tire Ed Sanders. It would take a full 30 years before the Swede was awarded his silver medal.

Johansson, born in Gothenburg on 16 October 1932, turned professional in 1952 and earned a reputation for hard-hitting punches. He was labelled the "Hammer of Thor" but it took him until 1960 to get a shot at the title. Floyd Patterson was his opponent and the bookies were confident that the underdog would not surprise them, especially as he hadn't been training particularly hard and was often seen out enjoying the nightlife. As it was, Johansson tore into Patterson, who was on the canvas seven times during the third round before the fight was stopped. The Swede's reign didn't last long,

◀ Ingemar Johansson fighting Floyd Patterson.

◀◀ Ingemar Johansson.

however, as Patterson gained his revenge in the rematch the following year.

Despite being floored in the first round, the challenger ended the bout in the sixth and Johansson retired two years later to become a successful businessman.

Johnson

For a man to become heavyweight champion of the world is an achievement in its own right; for Jack Johnson to achieve this in a world dominated by white men was unheard of...and hard for some to swallow. After Johnson had won the title in 1908, the boxing community launched a blatantly open campaign to find a white boxer who could defeat this "charlatan". To his credit, Johnson – who enjoyed dressing up as a "gentleman" to annoy his racist peers – took on all comers and ruled the roost until 1915.

Born in Galveston on 31 March 1878, John Arthur Johnson had never considered a career in boxing until he won a match at his local fair in 1897. He turned professional the same year and, rather than all out aggression, used a defensive stance waiting for his opponent to give him a clear shot. Johnson had to wait more than a decade before his shot at the title was no longer a race issue. He won a points decision over world champion Tommy Burns in December 1908 and successfully defended his title six times before losing it to Jess Willard who was hailed as a hero on his return. Hollywood offered him film roles as recompense for dethroning the black champion, such was the contempt felt by the majority of the country for Johnson in those difficult times.

The white community had even brought former champion James J Jeffries out of retirement in 1910 to

restore a white man to the pinnacle of the sport. "I am going into this fight for the sole purpose of proving that a white man is better than a Negro," was Jeffries' response when asked about his comeback. As it turned out, Jeffries hit the canvas twice during the fight before his corner threw in the towel. The aftermath of the fight on Independence Day saw riots across America as the white population struggled to come to terms with the result.

Johnson headed for Europe in exile from the US because of "morals charges" and did not return for many years even though at several points during his life he claimed to be homesick. Although Johnson never got another shot at the world title, he did fight sporadically until 1938. He died in a car accident in June 1946, before he had the opportunity to see the racial equality he so craved.

▲ Jack Johnson in action against Jess Willard.

◀ Jack Johnson, the first black world heavyweight champion.

Jones

▶ Roy Jones Jr celebrates after a bout against James Toney.

▶▶ Roy Jones Jr in action, 1995.

Named Fighter of the 1990s by the American Boxing Writers' Association, Roy Jones Jr is another who can claim to be regarded as one of the best pound for pound fighters ever. He has held world titles at middleweight, super middleweight, light heavyweight and heavyweight and can also boast to have held the WBC, WBA, IBF, IBO, WBF and IBA versions of the light heavyweight belt at the same time.

Roy Levesta Jones Jr was born in Florida on 16 January 1969 and represented the US at the 1988 Olympics in Seoul where he won the light middleweight silver medal before turning professional the following year. He captured the vacant IBF middleweight title with a unanimous points decision over Bernard Hopkins in May 1993 and hasn't looked back since.

Stepping up through the divisions, he has won super middleweight (1994), light heavyweight (1996) and heavyweight (2003) crowns during a glittering career. His first professional loss was against Montell Griffin in 1997, but he has since recorded another three (twice against Antonio Tarver and one to Glen Johnson) between 2004 and 2005. Since then he has returned to winning ways with victories over Prince Badi Ajamu, Anthony Hanshaw and Felix Trinidad.

Khan

Amir Khan took British boxing by storm with his performance at the 2004 Olympics in Athens. Virtually unheard of before then, Khan captured the public's attention as the country's sole boxing representative at the Games especially as he was only 17 at the time. He won the silver medal, losing in the final to Mario Kindelan – Khan would gain his revenge, defeating the Cuban in his final amateur fight in 2005.

The same year, Khan – born on 8 December 1986 – turned professional despite declaring an intention to go one step further and win gold at the 2008 Olympics. His career, however, was steered more carefully than that of his predecessor, Audley Harrison, who had promised so much after taking gold at the 2000 Olympics but whose professional career had faded into virtual obscurity.

Khan began with convincing performances and dispatched his opponents with consummate ease. The only time he had to go the distance in his first 15 outings was with Rachid Drilzane in December 2006. He won the Commonwealth

▲ Amir Khan poses with his silver medal at the Athens Olympics.

▲ Amir Khan (right) lands a blow as he defends his commonwealth crown against Gairy St Clair, February 2008.

lightweight title by beating Scott Lawton in October 2007 and, despite having to go to a points decision with Gairy St Clair in February 2008, looked set to become one of Britain's future world champions.

LaMotta

▶ Jake LaMotta in training.

▶▶ Jake LaMotta (left) and Marcel Cerdan exchange blows in their 1949 fight.

While many boxers emerged from the possibility of a life of crime to embrace fame and fortune in the ring, Jake LaMotta never really escaped the clutches of the criminals he associated with. He was constantly plagued by allegations of Mafia involvement in his fights and career path.

Nicknamed the "Bronx Bull" or the "Raging Bull", he was born Giacobbe La Motta in New York on 10 July 1921 and his life story was so interesting that it was made into a film, *Raging Bull* in 1980, starring Robert de Niro. LaMotta turned professional in 1941 but found himself with no hope of a shot at the world title until he agreed to throw a fight and accept a bribe.

Marcel Cerdan was the current middleweight champion but he proved no match for the aggressive LaMotta. Indeed, such was the ferocity of the American's attack that he dislocated Cerdan's shoulder when flinging him to the floor in June 1949. The Frenchman gamely continued but was unable to come out of his corner at the start of the 10th round and the belt was awarded to LaMotta. LaMotta successfully defended his title twice before being stopped by Sugar Ray Robinson in the 13th round in February 1951.

LaMotta retired in 1954 and took up an alternative career as a stand-up comedian.

Langford

Canadian Sam Langford has received many plaudits over the years but was never able to call himself champion of the world. ESPN called him "the greatest fighter nobody knows" while numerous writers described him as "one of the most talented boxers never to win the world championship".

Born on 12 February 1883 in Nova Scotia, Langford – like Jack Johnson – found racial prejudice an insurmountable obstacle to his ambition although he did take on Johnson in April 1906. With Johnson defending his world "coloured" heavyweight title, reports state that Langford gave the champion the fight of his life despite being knocked down in the sixth round. Langford recovered to finish the 15 round fight but it was Johnson who got the points decision.

It is alleged that Johnson feared Langford and refused to give him a rematch after becoming the first coloured world champion in 1908 but Johnson alleged that it was because Langford could not come up with the appropriate appearance fee. Nicknamed the "Boston Tar Baby", Langford turned professional in 1902 and fought over 300 bouts before retiring in 1926. He was soon blind and penniless but friends and fans raised money for him to live on until his death in January 1956.

◀ Sam Langford.

◀◀ Sam Langford who, despite continuing his boxing career until the age of 43, never took the world title.

Leonard

Hailed as one of the greatest lightweights ever to have lived, Benny Leonard had a superb talent that included the ability to hit his opponents hard while still concentrating on his technique. In all, Leonard fought more than 200 bouts, winning 183 with 70 of them by way of knockout.

Born in New York on 7 April 1896, Leonard was the son of Russian-Jewish parents and realised during street fights that he had a talent that could be nurtured and put to good use. He trained hard and turned professional in 1911 but had to wait until May 1917 to get his hands on his first world title. He floored lightweight champion Freddie Welsh three times in the ninth round and the fight was stopped. Leonard also contested the world welterweight title in June 1922 but was disqualified for punching holder Jack Britton while he was down on one knee.

Leonard remained undefeated until his first retirement in 1925 – supposedly because his mother told him to do so – but returned to the ring in 1931 having lost most of his money in the stock market crash of 1929. The years had not been kind to him, however, and he finally retired in 1932. Leonard later became a referee and was working when he suffered a massive heart attack and died in the ring in April 1947.

◀ Benny Leonard, one of the greatest lightweights of all time.

▼ Benny Leonard.

Leonard

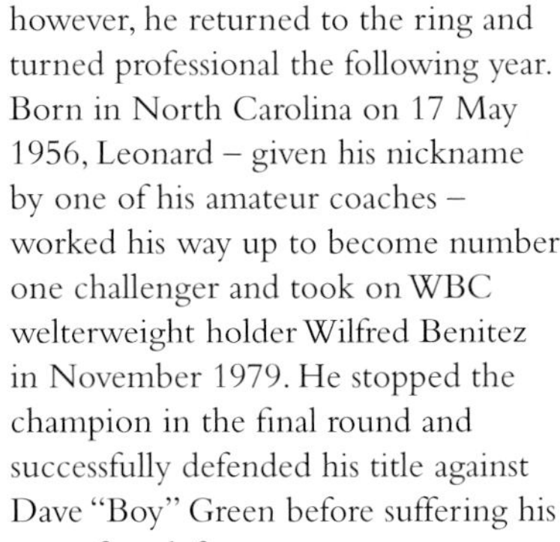

▶ Sugar Ray Leonard (right) and Roberto Duran go toe to toe during a bout in 1989.

▼ Sugar Ray Leonard in action at the Montreal Olympics, 1976.

The word "great" can be used far too liberally but it is the truth when used to describe Sugar Ray Leonard. Leonard though, did not intend to pursue a career in boxing although his ultimate goal eventually was to win Olympic gold which he achieved at the 1976 Games in Montreal before retiring.

Finding that money was tight, however, he returned to the ring and turned professional the following year. Born in North Carolina on 17 May 1956, Leonard – given his nickname by one of his amateur coaches – worked his way up to become number one challenger and took on WBC welterweight holder Wilfred Benitez in November 1979. He stopped the champion in the final round and successfully defended his title against Dave "Boy" Green before suffering his first defeat.

Leonard's bout with Roberto Duran has gone down in history as one of the most entertaining ever but the rematch three months later ended in bizarre circumstances with the Panamanian giving up in the eighth round.

Leonard went on to claim middleweight, super middleweight and light heavyweight crowns in a series of comebacks during the late 1980s. Having been involved in classic encounters with formidable adversaries such as Thomas Hearns and Marvin Hagler, Leonard's final comeback saw him lose to Hector Camacho in March 1997.

▲ A belt awarded to champion Lennox Lewis by the American Boxing magazine *Ring*.

▶ Lennox Lewis celebrating after beating Tony Tucker in 1993.

Lewis

Like so many others before and indeed after him, Lennox Lewis' first major success in boxing came when he won Olympic gold. Lewis – born on 2 September 1965 in London – moved to Canada at the age of 12 and it was there that he honed his skills. He represented his adopted nation at the 1984 Games in Los Angeles but had to settle for fifth place and vowed to return four years later. Instead of turning professional, he fulfilled his ambition and won the top prize in 1988, beating future world champion Riddick Bowe in the final in Seoul.

Lewis turned professional the following year and began a remarkable career that culminated in him becoming the first British boxer to

▲ Lennox Lewis lands a blow to the head of Oliver McCall during their WBC title fight, 1997.

be recognised as the undisputed heavyweight champion of the world for a century. He claimed the WBC crown from Tony Tucker in 1993 but unexpectedly lost to Oliver McCall the following year.

Regaining the vacant WBC title – ironically against McCall – Lewis added the WBA, IBF and IBO belts with a points decision over Evander Holyfield in 1999 in a rematch after a controversial draw. Lewis suffered his second defeat in April 2001, losing in an upset to Hasim Rahman but got his revenge in the return bout and was still a champion when he retired after fighting Vitali Klitschko in June 2003.

Lewis

Cited in the same league as boxers such as Jake LaMotta, Sugar Ray Leonard and Jim Corbett, Ted Lewis' style in the ring earned him fans wherever he fought. Preferring to go on the offensive, he rarely backed off his opponents, instead advancing with both fists in search of the knockout punch.

Born Gershon Mendeloff to Jewish parents in London on 24 October 1894, Lewis turned professional at the tender age of 14 and went on to fight 300 bouts. He signed off in 1929 with a career record of 228 victories (KO 80), 44 defeats (KO 5) and 23 draws, but not before becoming the undisputed welterweight champion of the world and becoming notable for making a mouth-guard commonplace.

His main adversary was American Jack Britton and, in August 1915, Lewis took his welterweight crown with a points decision after 12 rounds. In all, the pair would fight each other an incredible 20 times – six of them championship bouts. The title went to and fro between the pair from then up to 1919, but Lewis was having trouble with his weight. He

◀ Ted Lewis in training.

stepped up to light heavyweight and took on holder Georges Carpentier but was denied the title when the champion sneaked an illegal knockout punch while the referee was warning Lewis about holding. Lewis went on to become a popular coach and died in October 1970.

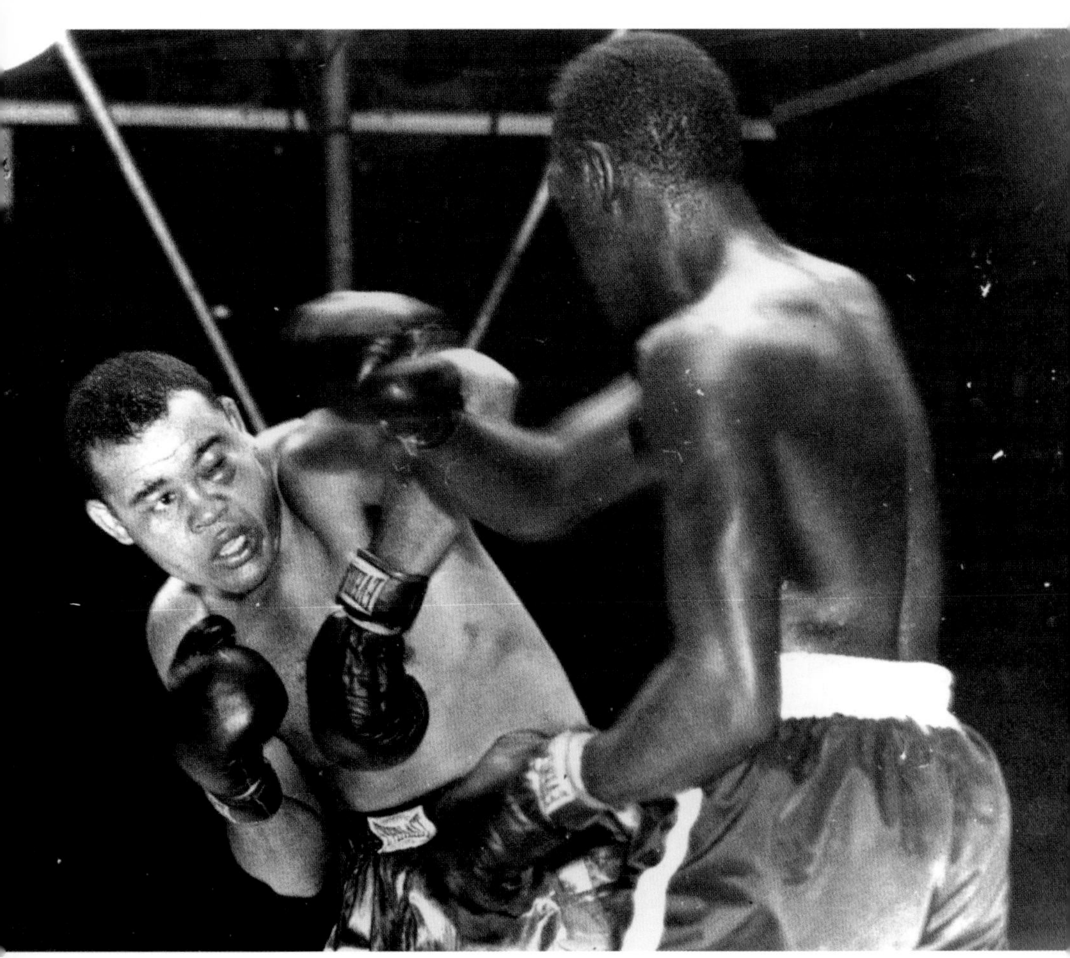

Louis

One of the greatest and most memorable boxers ever to have graced the ring was Joseph Louis Barrow, aka the "Brown Bomber". Born in Alabama on 13 May 1914, Louis – whose grandparents had been slaves in the deep South – was born into poverty and learned to box after his family moved to Detroit.

Turning professional in 1934, Louis quickly earned a reputation and was soon beating former heavyweight champions such as Primo Carnera and Max Baer, but Max Schmeling, another ex-title holder, studied the American's style and found a weakness in that Louis dropped his left low after jabbing. The German inflicted Louis' first defeat with a 12th round stoppage of the 1936 fight.

Louis contested the world heavyweight crown the following year and stopped James J Braddock in eight rounds to grab the belt. He went on to hold the title for more than a decade, making 25 successful defences (although the Second World War restricted his fights) before losing to Ezzard Charles in a comeback match in September 1950, 18 months after he had originally announced his retirement.

Louis fought on until the end of 1951 – contesting an incredible eight bouts in his final year – before retiring. Despite career earnings of some $5 million, Louis seemed to be perennially short of money and took various jobs offered to him by friends before his death in April 1981.

◀ With a swollen left eye, Joe Louis was on his way to defeat against Ezzard Charles.

▼ Joe Louis, one of the greatest prize fighters of all time.

Marciano

▶ Rocky Marciano who won 49 straight fights in his career.

▶▶ Rocky Marciano walks back to his corner after knocking out "Jersey" Joe Walcott.

The only heavyweight champion never to have been beaten as a professional, Rocky Marciano retired in 1955 with a career record of 49 victories from his 49 fights with an amazing 43 victories by way of knockout. Many have tried to emulate this feat, with Larry Holmes coming closest when he lost his 49th fight. The "Brockton Blockbuster" only contested 241 rounds during his 49 bouts, an average of less than five per fight.

Born in Massachusetts on 1 September 1923, Rocco Francis Marchegiano discovered his sporting prowess while still at school before joining the US Army during the Second World War. Initially considered too small to be a boxer, Marciano turned professional in 1947 and was contesting the world

title by September 1952. The reigning champion, "Jersey" Joe Walcott, survived for 13 rounds as Marciano claimed the crown but the rematch was over almost before it began with Walcott being knocked out in the first round.

Marciano went on to defend his title another five times – including two bouts against Ezzard Charles – before retiring in September 1955. He died the day before his 46th birthday when the light plane he was travelling in crashed in bad weather in Des Moines, Iowa, in August 1969.

Mayweather

▲ Floyd Mayweather Jr celebrates after defeating Arturo Gatti in 2005.

One of the great fighters of the current generation, Floyd Mayweather Jr's family can boast a long tradition of world champion boxers. While his father never won a world title, two of his uncles between them reached the pinnacle of the super featherweight, light welterweight and welterweight divisions.

Born Floyd Joy Sinclair (his mother's surname) in Michigan on 24 February 1977, Mayweather Jr was ranked the number one pound for pound boxer in the world in the mid-2000s by *Ring* magazine. He turned professional in 1996 and has since won world titles in five different divisions.

His first crown came in October 1998 with an eighth round stoppage of WBC super featherweight champion Genaro Hernandez. Four years later, he successfully made the transition to lightweight and claimed José Luis Castillo's WBC belt before stripping Arturo Gatti of his WBC light welterweight title in June 2005. The following year saw him win welterweight titles after beating Zab Judah and Carlos Baldomir and in May 2007, he defeated Oscar De La Hoya for the WBC light middleweight crown.

Mayweather Jr retained his WBC welterweight title with a 10th round stoppage of the previously undefeated Ricky Hatton in December 2007 and – without a loss in his first 39 fights – shocked his fans by announcing his retirement in June 2008 at the age of 31.

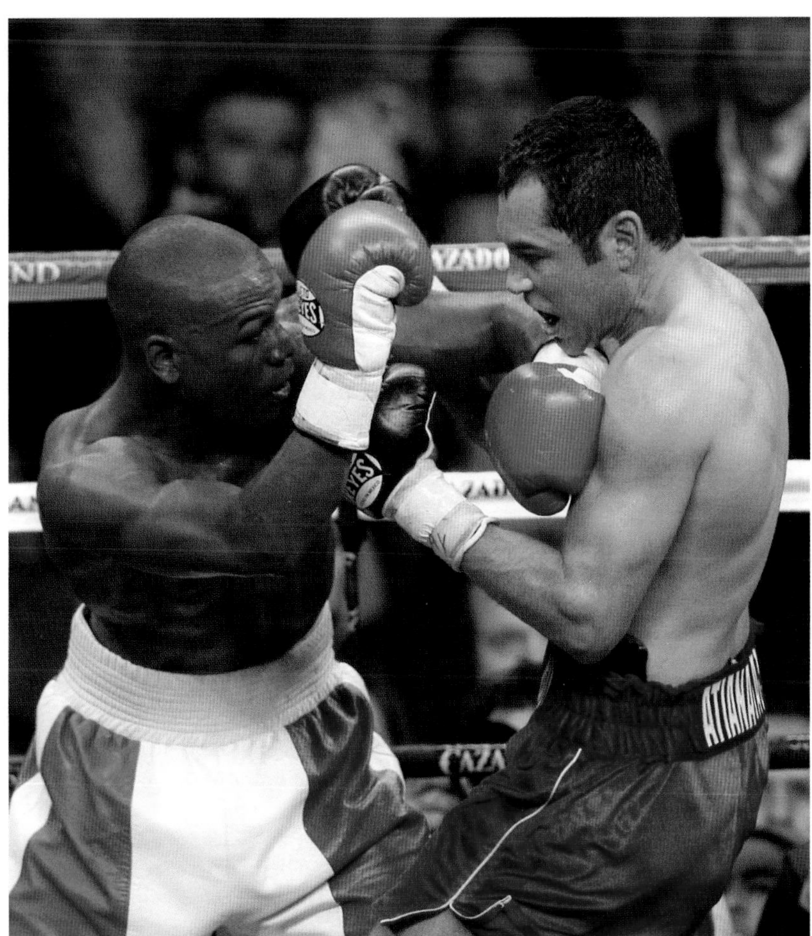

◀ Floyd Mayweather Jr lands a punch on Oscar De La Hoya during a fight in 2007.

McGuigan

▼ Barry McGuigan in action against WBA champion Eusebio Pedroza.

Barry McGuigan achieved what many before him had tried – to unite both Republicans and Loyalists in his native Ireland. Born Finbar Patrick McGuigan – the son of a famous Irish singer – on 28 February 1961, the "Clones Cyclone" (derived from the town of his birth) suffered an early setback in his career when he lost on points to Peter Eubanks in August 1981 (brother of future super middleweight champion Chris) in only his third outing.

Having turned professional that year, McGuigan needed to get his career back on track and this he did, winning his next 18 bouts (although tragedy occurred in June 1982 when his opponent, Young Ali, spent months in a coma after his sixth round knockout and eventually died from brain injuries received in the fight). McGuigan challenged WBA featherweight champion Eusebio Pedroza in June 1985 inflicting the Panamanian's first defeat in seven years to claim the title.

McGuigan succumbed to a points defeat in his third title defence, against Steve Cruz in June 1986, and took a two year hiatus before returning to the ring. He never again contested a world title fight and retired in May 1989, preferring instead to commentate on boxing rather than participate.

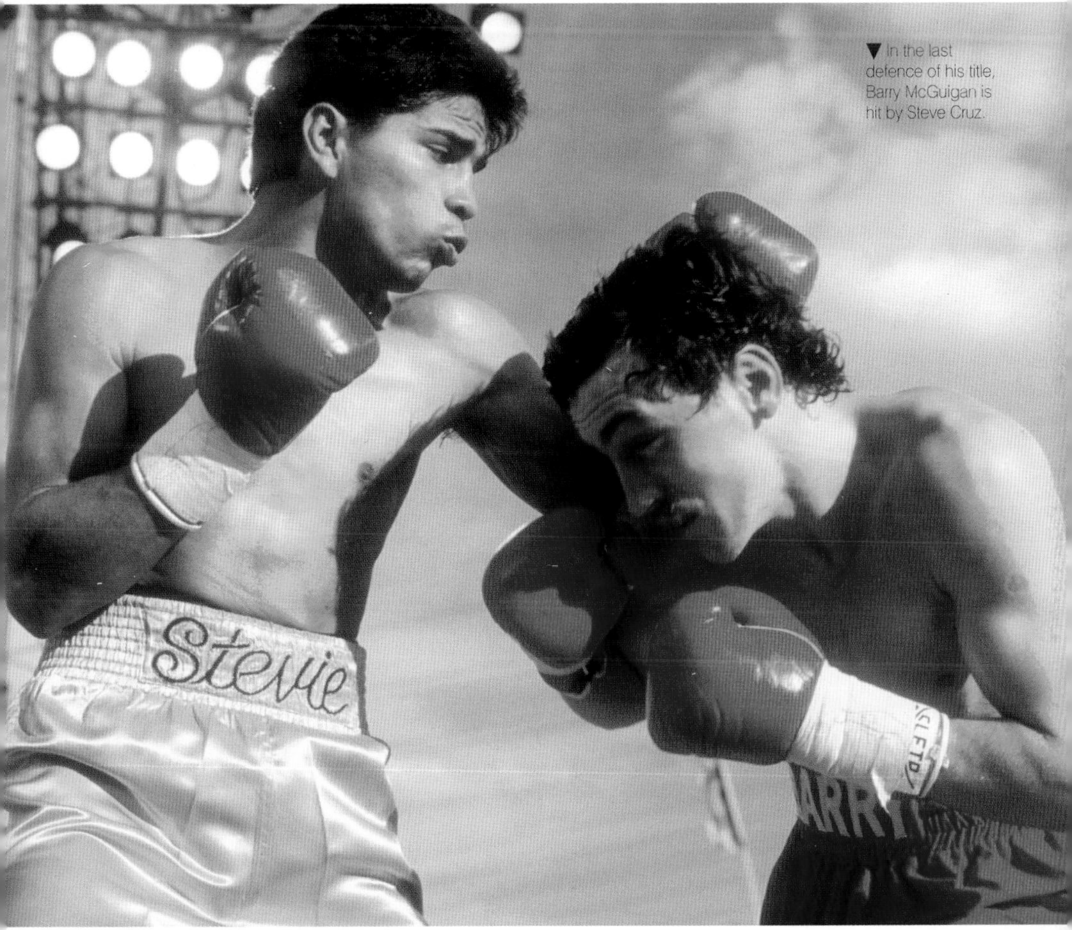

▼ In the last defence of his title, Barry McGuigan is hit by Steve Cruz.

Mills

One of the bravest – though not particularly technically gifted – boxers that ever graced the ring, Freddie Mills was also extremely popular with fight fans. His route to becoming a professional took an unusual turn when he signed up to take on all comers in a fairground booth but he began his career proper with a first round knockout of Jim Riley in February 1936.

Born on 26 June 1919 in Parkstone, Dorset, Mills won his only world title when he stopped Len Harvey in the second round of their light heavyweight contest in February 1942. He lost the best years of his career to the Second World War and found himself serving in the RAF when he was in his prime. Mills contested two more world title bouts; against Gus Lesnevich that was stopped in the 10th round in May 1946, and his final outing against Joey Maxim in January 1950 that ended in identical circumstances.

Retiring after the Maxim fight, Mills invested in a restaurant and befriended London gangsters the Kray twins. He was found dead in his car on 25 July 1965 with a gunshot wound to his head. Suspicion still surrounds his death today and theories range from suicide to gangland killing.

◀◀ Freddie Mills celebrates after his world light heavyweight title victory over Gus Lesnevich.

◀ Freddie Mills was not the most stylish of boxers.

▲ Archie Moore had one of the longest professional careers in the history of the sport.

► Archie Moore.

Moore

Archie Moore is credited as being the boxer who holds the record for the most number of wins by knockout, although figures vary between 131 and 145. Nicknamed the "Old Mongoose", he is also claimed to have fought under the alias "Fourth of July Kid" so his true record may never be known with any certainty. Even the exact date of his birth is clouded with uncertainty – he insists he was born on 13 December

1916 in Mississippi but his mother states that she gave birth to him three years earlier.

Whatever the truth, Moore was born Archibald Lee Wright and turned professional in 1935, but he had to wait 17 years before he won his first world title. Paired with light heavyweight champion Joey Maxim, Moore won a unanimous decision in December 1952. There would be two rematches over the next couple of years with the same outcome.

Moore defended his title on another seven occasions, winning his final light heavyweight championship bout with Giulio Rinaldi in June 1961 (the NBA had stripped him of his title because of "inactivity" although other organisations still recognised him as the champion). Moore even stepped up to contest the heavyweight championship with Rocky Marciano in September 1955 (Moore was stopped in the ninth round) and Floyd Patterson the following year (this time, he failed to make it past the fifth round). Having retired in 1963, Archie Moore died of heart failure in San Diego in December 1998.

Nelson

▶ Azumah Nelson celebrates after a bout against Jeff Fenech.

▶▶ Azumah Nelson and Jesse James Leija trade blows.

Although Azumah Nelson had been boxing professionally since 1979, it was only when he was called up as a late substitute for a WBC featherweight bout in July 1982 that he became known – and his abilities recognised – outside his native Ghana. Born on 19 September 1958, Nelson lost against champion Salvador Sanchez by a knockout in the last round but he had, at last, arrived on the world stage.

Galvanised by this defeat, Nelson resumed his career with six straight victories before taking on then WBC featherweight holder Wilfredo Gomez in December 1984. This time, he made no mistake and dethroned the champion in the 11th round. He successfully defended his crown six times before stepping up to take on Mario Azabache Martinez for the vacant WBC super featherweight title in 1988. This time, he was forced to

go the distance but won a split decision.

Nelson moved up a division to challenge at lightweight, losing to Pernell Whitaker in May 1990 and Jesse James Leija in July 1998 (after which he retired). Nelson met Leija four times in the final five years of his career with the pair registering two victories apiece. In all, Nelson's career record saw him win 39 (KO 28), lose five (KO 1) and draw two of his fights, and he retired back to Ghana a national hero.

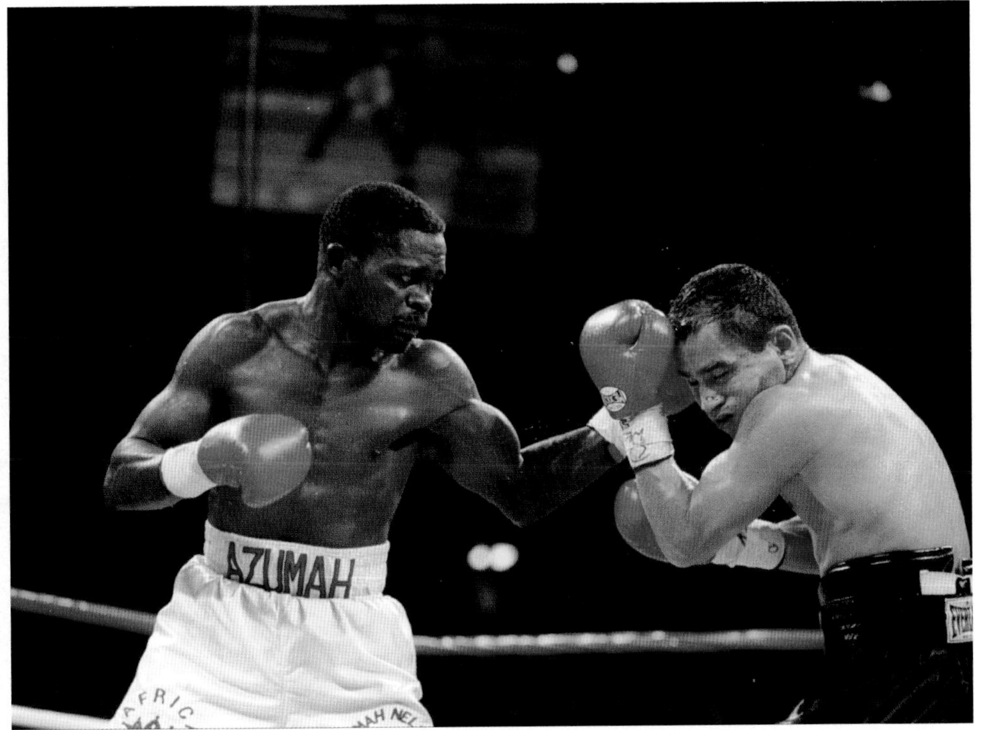

Olivares

▼ Ruben Olivares stands over Lionel Rose after smashing him to the canvas.

Perhaps the best boxer to emerge from Mexico, Ruben Olivares has been described by many as the best bantamweight ever.

He won 88 of his 104 bouts, 77 of them by knockout, and had two spells wearing the bantamweight crown as well as two as featherweight champion.

Born in Mexico City on 14 January 1947, Olivares turned professional in 1964 and began a run of 22 consecutive knockouts. By the time he challenged WBC and WBA bantamweight champion Lionel Rose in August 1969, Olivares' record read 51 wins and 1 draw. By the time that bout ended, Olivares had added another knockout and claimed his first world title. After defending his belt against Alan Rudkin, Olivares then had three championship showdowns with fellow Mexican Chucho Castillo during 1970 and 1971. The first ended in a unanimous decision for Olivares, the second saw the champion stopped with a cut over the eye in the 14th round, while the third saw a repeat of the first bout. Two more defences followed before Olivares surrendered his title to Rafael Herrera with an eighth round stoppage in March 1972.

Olivares' next world title fight was for the vacant WBA featherweight title two years later and he knocked out Zensuke Utagawa in the seventh

▼ Ruben Olivares in action.

round. His reign was ended by Alexis Arguello, but he regained his title from Bobby Chacon only to lose it again, this time to David Kotey…all in the space of a year! One more unsuccessful title challenge was to follow, against Eusebio Pedroza in July 1979 before Olivares hung up his gloves in 1981. He made single-fight comebacks in 1986 and 1988 before finally retiring.

Pep

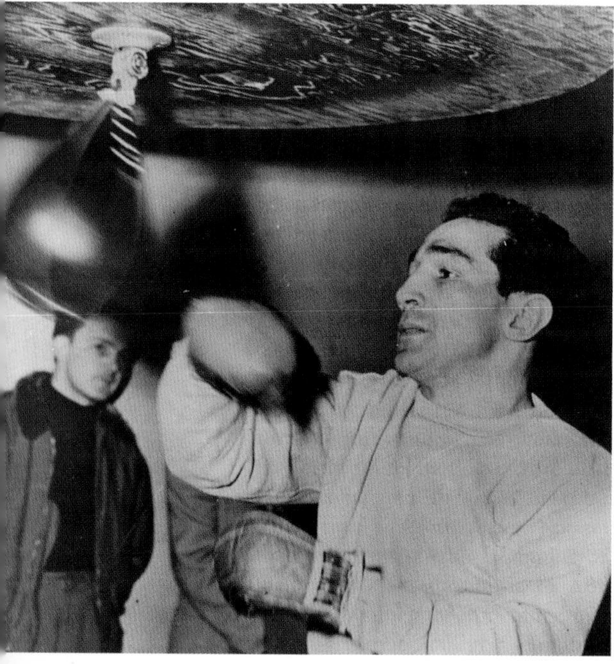

Frankly, it will be a miracle if another featherweight comes anywhere near matching the record that Willie Pep set in the mid-20th century. He contested 241 fights, winning 229 (KO 65), losing 11 (KO 6) and drawing once before finally hanging up his gloves in 1966.

Born Guglielmo Papaleo in Connecticut on 19 September 1922, Pep turned professional in 1940 and quickly racked up victories in his first 62 fights. In November 1942, Pep stood toe-to-toe for 15 rounds with world featherweight champion Chalky Wright to claim his first title by unanimous decision. In an era when boxers didn't tend to put their titles on the line in every fight, it didn't matter too much that Pep lost to Sammy Angott by a dubious decision in March 1943 because he held on to his crown until losing to Sandy Saddler in February 1949. Pep – nicknamed "Will O'The Wisp" – reclaimed his title in the rematch the following year but lost again to Saddler in February 1950.

In fact, Saddler proved to be his nemesis as he denied Pep another world title in September 1951 in what turned out to be Pep's last shot at winning a third championship. Pep retired in 1959

◀ Willie Pep in action against Jimmy Connors in 1957.

◀◀ Willie Pep in training.

– making a brief comeback between 1965 and 1966 – before becoming an inspector and referee. Willie Pep died on 23 November 2006.

Queensberry Rules

▶ Sir John Sholto Douglas Queensberry after whom the Queensberry rules were named.

While boxing has been around for thousands of years in one form or another, the modern sport can trace its roots back to 1743 with the introduction of the London Prize Ring rules. A revised version of these rules was published in 1853 but was soon superseded by the Queensberry rules in 1867, so called because they were publicly endorsed by the ninth Marquess of Queensberry – John Douglas (1844-1900).

Written by John Graham Chambers, a major figure in the development of boxing and athletics in the UK, the code persuaded boxers not to "fight simply to win; no holds barred is not the way, you must win by the rules".

Stipulations included; that the dimensions of the ring should be 24 feet (or as near as possible), no wrestling or hugging, the duration of and rest time

◀ The ninth Marquess of Queensberry publicly endorsed the sport's new rules in 1897.

between rounds, allowing a fallen boxer 10 seconds to regain his feet unaided, the required use of appropriate boxing gloves, pointing out that a man on one knee should be considered "down" and therefore not be punched, and – perhaps most bizarrely – that shoes or boots with springs would not be allowed.

Reid

▶ Robin Reid with his belts.

▶▶ Sugar Ray Robinson was a dominant force in the ring for two decades.

Robin Reid may well have been a world super middleweight champion but he couldn't please everyone and his critics claim that he lacked the killer punch…although he recorded knockouts in 27 of his 39 victories. Despite this apparent "weakness", he was extremely popular with British fight fans.

Born in Sefton on 19 July 1971, Reid turned professional in 1993 and had won 21 of his first 22 fights (the other ended in a draw) when he came to face Vincenzo Nardiello for the WBC title in October 1996. He stopped the Italian in seven rounds to claim the belt and went on to enjoy three successful defences before losing a unanimous decision to Thulani Malinga the following year.

Unsuccessful championship bouts followed against Joe Calzaghe and Silvio Branco before he scored a first round knockout of Mike Gormley for the vacant WBF title in December 2000. Reid defended his title five times over the next two years – including against Julio Cesar Vasquez – but failed to claim Sven Ottke's IBF and WBA belts in December 2003. Although Reid triumphed in his IBO showdown with Brian Magee the following June, August 2005 saw him competing for a world title for the final time. Jeff Lacy stopped the "Grim Reaper" in the seventh round and, after two 2007 bouts, Reid hung up his gloves.

Robinson

Born Walker Smith Jr on 3 May 1921, "Sugar" Ray Robinson is frequently cited as one of the greatest boxers of all time. It is unclear whether the great fighter's actual birthplace was in Georgia or Michigan, but what are not in doubt are his exceptional performances as a welterweight and middleweight. Robinson won all his amateur matches (85 in total) where 69 were knockout victories. He turned professional in 1940 at the age of 19 and went on to hold the world welterweight championship between 1946 and 1951.

By this time, Robinson had amassed 128 wins (with 84 knockouts) and had only been defeated on one occasion. He also won the world middleweight title in 1951 but retired in 1952. However, by 1955, Robinson was back in the ring and he regained his middleweight title. It was a crown he would defend five times (the first time a boxer had done so). He was named "The Greatest Fighter of the 20th Century" by Associated Press and he was rated the best "pound for pound"

▶ Sugar Ray Robinson's fight against his countryman Jake LaMotta.

boxer of all time in 1997 by *Ring* magazine. Robinson was inducted into the International Boxing Hall of Fame in 1967. The flamboyant boxer retired from the sport in 1965 and died in Los Angeles on 12 April 1989.

Saddler

▲ Willie Pep with Joseph "Sandy" Saddler in 1949.

Joseph "Sandy" Saddler was twice world featherweight champion and a former junior lightweight winner. Born on 23 June 1926 in Boston, Massachusetts, Saddler's career spanned 12 years between 1944 and 1956. Of his total 163 professional fights, he claimed 145 wins (of which 103 were knockouts), suffered 16 defeats and drew matches on two occasions. He was only ever stopped in a bout once, against Jock Leslie. It was his second professional fight.

Saddler had a prolific four-bout series with the legendary Willie Pep, which began on 29 October 1948. Pep, who was the current world featherweight champion, was little disturbed by his match against Saddler having racked up 134 wins out of a total of 136 matches. Pep had enjoyed a winning streak since 1943 when his last defeat had come at the hands of Sammy Angott who beat the reigning champion by decision. But, Pep was to find his match in Saddler who knocked his fellow American down four times before winning a fourth round knockout victory.

Saddler then lost the world title back to Pep on points over 15 rounds on 11 February 1949 in one of the most exciting matches in the history of the sport. A year later, and Saddler again became title holder when he regained the crown by a technical knockout in the eighth round on 8 September 1950. He retired from boxing in 1956 following an eye injury sustained in an accident and later trained George Foreman. He died on 18 September 2001.

Schmeling

▶ Max Schmeling.

German boxer Maximilian Adolph Otto Siegfried Schmeling was born on 28 September 1905 in Klein Luckow in the Province of Pomerania. He was widely regarded as a Nazi sympathiser, however, he risked his own life to save two German-Jewish children in 1938. He was world heavyweight champion between 1930 and 1932.

Schmeling's professional debut came in 1924 and he clocked up an impressive 42 wins (with only four defeats and three draws) before facing Jack Sharkey for the vacant world title in 1930. However, the win was not complete glory for Schmeling, who effectively won the title because of Sharkey's disqualification with a low, severe blow which saw the German unable to continue the bout. It was the first and last time that the heavyweight championship was won in this way. Two years later and the two boxers met for a rematch. Sharkey was declared the winner after 15 rounds on points but Schmeling's manager, Joe Jacobs, was so outraged by the win that he was heard to shout "We was robbed", a quote that has since become famous the world over.

In 1936, Schmeling handed Joe Louis his first ever defeat at a match in New York. It had been thought that the American was unbeatable and Louis

was devastated by the professional blow. They met again for a rematch in June 1938 and, this time, Louis defended his crown with a technical knockout in the first round. Adolph Hitler took the defeat of Schmeling as an embarrassment to Germany and the German boxer was wrongly labelled a Nazi. He retired in 1948 and died on 2 February 2005.

▲ Max Schmeling shakes hands with Joe Louis while being weighed in before one of their fights.

Sullivan

▶ John L Sullivan the last bare knuckle heavyweight champion.

▶▶ Gene Tunney wearing protective headgear, 1923.

John Lawrence Sullivan was the first heavyweight champion of bare knuckle fighting between 1882 and 1892. Born on 15 October 1858 in Massachusetts, his family hailed from County Kerry in Ireland. The part of Massachusetts where Sullivan was born, Roxbury, later became a part of Boston and he was quickly nicknamed the "Boston Strong Boy". He became renowned for being arrested during his youth for fighting in parts of the country where boxing was outlawed and would often travel on exhibition tours where he would offer people money to fight him.

Between 1883 and 1884, Sullivan travelled with five other knuckle boxers across the country to give 195 performances. During the tour, Sullivan knocked out 11 men after fighting under the Queensberry rules. There were no formal boxing titles at the time, but he is widely regarded as the first world champion following his victories over Paddy Ryan and Charley Mitchell.

Sullivan received his first belt on 8 August 1887 but found his match in Mitchell in an illegal match in Chantilly, France. Mitchell was arrested for unlawful fighting, but Sullivan managed to evade the gendarmes and was quickly ferried back across the Channel where he convalesced in Liverpool. When Sullivan faced Jake Kilrain on 7 July 1889 fighting under the London Prize rules, it was the last official bare knuckle fight in boxing history. He retired in the 1890s and died on 2 February 1918.

Tunney

James Joseph Tunney, better known as Gene, was nicknamed the "Fighting Marine". Born on 25 May 1897, in New York City, Tunney was the heavyweight champion between 1926 and 1928 and was legendary for beating Jack Dempsey on two occasions, in 1926 and 1927. His nickname, unsurprisingly, came from the fact that Tunney was a US marine who served his country in the First World War.

Two particular matches make Tunney one of the most renowned boxers of his generation. First, was his impressive bout against Dempsey which became one of the most famous in boxing history and is known as "The Long Count Fight" and second, was the fact that Tunney was only defeated once in his career. Dempsey was the most famous fighter of the era and Tunney's two time defeats of the

▲ Gene Tunney flexing his muscles.

reigning champion were attributed to his quick thinking and his ability to turn any boxing match into a game.

The thought processes which Tunney deployed were likened more to a game of chess than fighting in a ring and it was not a particularly popular style at a time when slugging it out against the top flight fighters such as Dempsey, Harry Greb and Mickey Walker was all the rage. However, Tunney was influenced by the likes of other boxers who thought through their matches including Benny Leonard and James J Corbett. His only defeat came against Greb for the American light heavyweight title in a 15 round unanimous decision. He avenged the loss with four wins over Greb before retiring from boxing in 1928. He died at the age of 81 on 7 November 1978.

Turpin

Better known as the "Leamington Licker", Randolph Adolphus Turpin was born on 7 June 1928 in Leamington Spa. He was to become one of Europe's most prolific middleweight boxers of the 1940s and 1950s. Turpin turned professional in 1946, just after his 18th birthday, and knocked Gordon Griffiths out in the first round of his debut. He went on to win a further 16 times before he drew in a match against Mark Hart in 1947.

After three more victories, Turpin was set to face Albert Finch, who delivered the young boxer his first defeat in an eighth round stoppage. However, with his winning streak firmly in place, Turpin was pitched against the world middleweight champion Sugar Ray Robinson. On 10 July 1951, Turpin snatched the world title from the undisputed champion and found himself an instant national hero. But, Turpin's reign would not last long and he lost the crown to Robinson in a technical knockout in the 10th round of their rematch in New York.

It seemed to be the turning point in Turpin's fortunes and, although he went on to beat Don Cockell to claim the British Commonwealth light heavyweight championship, his return to New York saw the former champion defeated at the hands of Bobo Olson in 15 rounds. He then lost his European middleweight title and by 1958 his best boxing days were over. He retired with 66 wins, eight losses and one draw. Turpin died on 17 May 1966.

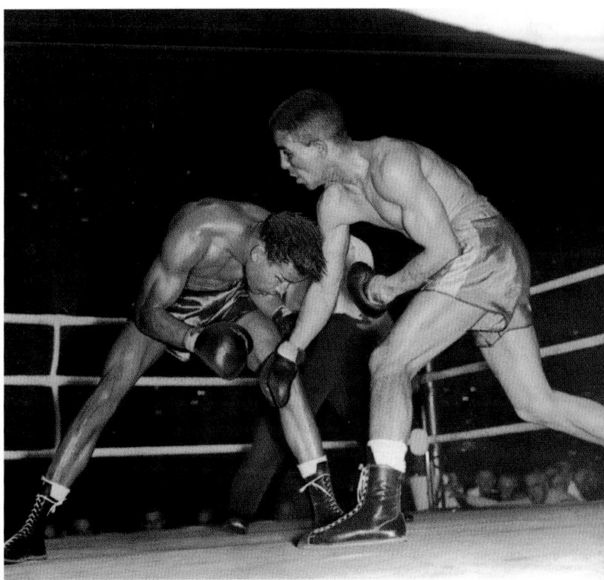

▲ Turpin was the underdog in this fight against Sugar Ray Robinson.

Tyson

Born on 30 June 1966, Mike Tyson is one of the most famous boxers that has ever lived. Nicknamed "Iron" Mike Tyson, "Kid Dynamite" and the "Baddest Man on the Planet", Tyson was a force to be reckoned with in the ring. Impressively, Tyson won two world heavyweight championships during his long career and is still the youngest man to have won the title.

Renowned for his controversial behaviour as much outside the ring as in it, Tyson endured three years in prison where he converted to Islam and changed his name to Malik Abdul Aziz. But, on his release, Tyson was back and, in 1997, famously bit off a portion of his opponent's ear in a fight against Evander Holyfield. At the age of 35 he once again contended for the title, but was knocked out by Lennox Lewis in 2002.

Expelled from school for fighting, Tyson – who hails from Brooklyn, New York – spent much of his youth in and out of juvenile detention centres where his talent was spotted and encouraged by former boxer

Bobby Stewart who introduced the young boy to manager and trainer Cus D'Amato. He became Tyson's guardian and Kid Dynamite was then trained by Kevin Rooney and Teddy Atlas. Rooney would eventually become Tyson's full-time trainer and manager.

His amateur career took off in style where he proved himself as a formidable opponent and turned professional in 1984. He defeated Hector Mercedes in a knockout in the first round on his debut in 1985 and won 19 of his first 22 fights by knockouts. His first stab at the heavyweight title came in 1986 when he beat Trevor Berbick by a technical knockout in the second round. At just 20 years old, Tyson became the youngest man ever to win the prestigious belt and was renowned for his incredible strength. In fact, many boxers were intimidated by Tyson and he became an undisputed world champion.

But, expectations of the young New Yorker were high and his problems outside the ring were beginning to hit the headlines. He fired long-time trainer Rooney which ultimately saw the demise of Tyson's highly honed skills and he became prone to looking for the one punch knockout rather than fighting a good match. By 1990, it all looked to be going rapidly downhill for Tyson and he lost the championship to James "Buster" Douglas in Tokyo on 11 February. During the match, Tyson was knocked to the canvas for the first time in his career, causing a great deal of upset in the boxing fraternity. After his comeback in 1995, Tyson eventually retired from boxing in 2005, however, he continues to give exhibition bouts in boxing tours across the US.

◀ Evander Holyfield and Mike Tyson trade punches during their WBA heavyweight championship fight.

▼ Mike Tyson raises his hands in celebration following his victory over Bruce Seldon.

Ulrich

▶ Thomas Ulrich with the European light heavyweight belt.

One time Olympic medal winner Thomas Ulrich was born on 11 July 1975 in Berlin, Germany. His amateur highlights were numerous and his first real triumph came in 1992 at the junior world championships in Montreal, Canada, where he claimed second prize. He had defeated South Korean Jae-Yeol and Willard Lewis of Canada for the prestigious award. Ulrich went on to become the German light heavyweight champion in 1994.

The following year, he followed up his triumph with a bronze medal in the light heavyweight bouts at the world amateur championships held in Berlin. Ulrich defeated Yevgeny Makarenko of Russia, Mohamed Benguesmia of Algeria and Timur Ibragimov of Uzbekistan to claim his medal. However, it was his performance at the 1996 Olympic Games in Atlanta that brought his widespread recognition. Ulrich walked away with the bronze medal in the light heavyweight division having successfully defeated Australian Rick Timperi and Ismael Kone from Sweden. Despite also defeating Daniel Bispo from Brazil, he lost one fight to Seung-Bae Lee of South Korea. It wasn't enough to rob the German of his Olympic medal.

He turned professional in 1997 and was given a shot at the WBC light heavyweight title against title holder Tomasz Adamek in 2005. Defeated in his quest, Ulrich attempted to gain the WBO light heavyweight championship but lost by a decision to Zsolt Erdei.

Vasquez

Julio Cesar Vasquez is best known for winning the WBA junior middleweight championship. Born on 13 July 1966 in Santa Fe, Argentina, Vasquez soon coined the nickname "El Zurdo" for his ability to lead with his left, rather than his right hand. The southpaw turned professional in 1986 and won the vacant title in 1992 when he knocked out the little known Hitoshi Kamiyama from Japan.

Vasquez went on to successfully defend his title 10 times, beating the likes of Javier Castillejo and Aaron "Superman" Davis. He also defended the title against the, until then, undefeated Tony Marshall and Winky Wright, but he lost the belt to the legendary Pernell Whitaker three years later. Despite the disappointment, Vasquez went on to claim the WBA light middleweight title from Carl Daniels, also renowned for being a prominent lefty, by knocking his opponent out with a single left in the 11th round. Despite having trailed on points, this was named *Ring* magazine's Knockout of the Year in 1995 but Vasquez would lose the title in his next fight to Laurent Boudouani. Following his knockout defeat, Vasquez decided not to contend the title again, however, he continues to box in his native country.

▲ Julio Cesar Vasquez celebrating after his fight against Armand Picar.

Walcott

▶ Action from the fight between Joe Walcott and Joe Louis.

Born on 31 January 1914, Arnold Raymond Cream was destined to become a heavyweight champion. When his father died when Cream was just 13 years old, he gave up his schooling and worked in a soup factory to support his mother and 11 brothers and sisters. He also took up boxing and adopted the name of his idol, Joe Walcott, and became known himself as "Jersey" Joe after the state of New Jersey in which he was born.

His debut against Cowboy Wallace came on 9 September 1930 which he won in a knockout in round one. He then had a further five knockout victories before he tasted his first defeat against Henry Wilson who won the bout on points. He amassed a record of 44 wins before challenging for the world title. As a heavyweight, Jersey Joe would beat Joe Baksi and Lee Q Murray, Curtis Sheppard and Jimmy Bivins before he faced Joe Louis in the title match. He was, at the time, the oldest man to try for the heavyweight championship at the age of 33.

Walcott knocked Louis down in the first and fourth rounds, but lost on a split decision. As most of the boxing fraternity and spectators thought Walcott should have won, a rematch was scheduled on 25 June 1948. Again he lost to Louis and then later to Ezzard Charles. However, determined to try again, Walcott was rewarded when he won the heavyweight championship on 18 July 1951 with a seventh round stoppage of Charles. Joe later became a referee and died on 25 February 1994.

Walker

Boxing legend Mickey Walker, from New Jersey, was born Edward Patrick Walker on 13 July 1901. Nicknamed the "Toy Bulldog", Walker was a welterweight and middleweight champion and was fearless in his matches against light heavyweights and heavyweights alike. Together with his manager, Jack "Doc" Kearns, Walker was ready to take on any opponent at any time despite being only 5' 7" tall.

His first title came in 1922 when he defeated the current welterweight champion Jack Britton, and then successfully enjoyed defences against Lew Tendler, Jimmy Jones, Bobby Barrett and Pete Latzo. He later lost the championship to Latzo in 1926 but was soon back at the top when he won the middleweight championship from holder Tiger Flowers.

By 1931, however, Walker was predominantly fighting heavyweights and gave up his middleweight title. Despite impressive bouts with Tommy Loughran, Johnny Risko and Bearcat Wright, Walker would never hold a heavyweight title. He was renowned for his strong and rugged approach and his exceptional stamina.

When he retired from boxing in 1939, Walker opened a popular restaurant in New York and became an accomplished artist. He was also a keen golfer and was inducted into the International Boxing Hall of Fame in 1990. He had died just nine years before on 28 April 1981.

▼ Mickey Walker.

Wilde

▶ Jimmy Wilde was a great flyweight.

Known by a variety of names including "Mighty Atom", the "Ghost with the Hammer in his Hand" and "Tylorstown Terror", Welshman Jimmy Wilde is considered by some to be the "greatest flyweight ever". Wilde was a slightly built man who could box way above his own weight and was renowned for his devastating punch. Even the legendary American heavyweight Gene Tunney described Wilde as "The best fighter I ever saw".

His first professional match came on 26 December 1910 against Les Williams and ended in a no-decision after three rounds. However, his first win came less than a month later when he defeated Ted Roberts in the third round on 1 January 1911. For 103 bouts, Wilde would remain undefeated until, challenging Tancy Lee for the European championship, he would find himself knocked out in the 17th round.

But it did little to deter the eight-stone Welshman who took the title from flyweight champion Joe Symonds in the 12th round on 14 February 1916. He retained his title in 1917 beating challenger George Clarke. The win also brought him the European title and recovered the British title that he had lost to Tancy Lee. He also went on to defend his world title against Lee and exacted his revenge with a knockout in the 11th round. After a successful career with a staggering 99 knockout victories, Wilde retired to Barry, South Wales, where he died on 10 March 1969.

Williams

Although he is mostly forgotten today, Ike Williams is considered one of the top 10 all time lightweights in any list. Born on 2 August 1923, in Brunswick, Georgia in the United States, Williams became the NBA world lightweight champion in April 1945 when he defeated rival Juan Zurita for the title. For most of his career, Williams was managed by the infamous Mafia boss Blinky Palermo, who "owned" Sonny Liston, although he tried convincing the boxing managers' guild that he could manage himself.

Although Williams was called by the Kefauver Commission to confirm that he had never thrown any fights for Palermo, he did claim that he took a dive in a match against Chuck Davey. He also claimed that Palermo took most of the boxer's money. Williams was notable for defeating high profile names in the business including the likes of Sammy Angott, also known as "The Clutch", and Bob "Bobcat" Montgomery. He also defeated the legendary Beau Jack, twice winner of the world title. Williams was named in the 2003 *Ring* magazine list as one of the 100 greatest punchers of all time and was the magazine's Ring Fighter of 1948. He died at the age of 71 on 5 September 1994.

▲ Ike Williams was known for his great right hand.

XXX Rated Fights

▲ Michael Watson and Chris Eubank.

Boxing is a highly revered sport and has many fans the world over. It is dangerous and exciting, but many doctors, amongst others, have called for the sport to be banned. Cuts and bruises are the most common injuries sustained in the ring, but dental work and internal bleeding are just as likely. The ultimate price paid by any boxer is with their life.

The quiet and unassuming Welshman Johnny Owen (7 January 1956 – 4 November 1980) was one such boxer. The Welsh, British, Commonwealth and European bantamweight champion lost his own fight for life having suffered horrendous injuries and falling into a coma in a match against Lupe Pintor for the world championship. He was just 24 years old.

Another boxer who found out the hard way exactly how harsh boxing could be is Michael Watson (born 15 March 1965) who met Chris Eubank in a rematch for the world middleweight title in September 1991. During the final bout, referee Roy Francis put himself between Eubank's punches and Watson's head but the boxer collapsed soon after. He went without oxygen for a staggering 30 minutes as no medical staff were on standby. He spent 40 days in a coma and underwent six operations to remove a clot from his brain. Despite his doctor's prognosis Watson fought back to learn how to eat, walk and talk again and in 2003, he became a national hero when he completed the London Marathon despite it taking him six days.

Yamaguchi

WBA light flyweight champion Keiji Yamaguchi was born in Hakodate, Japan, on 17 February 1974. The Japanese champion – just 5' 5½" tall – was discovered by legendary promoter Hiroaki Tsuda, who had transformed his small home into a training facility to cultivate the career of superstar Hidekazu Akai.

Having failed in his ambitions with the likes of Hiroki Ioka and Masamori Tokuyama, Tsuda turned his attentions to Yamaguchi who won the 108-pound belt with his quick skill against Carlos Murillo from Panama with a unanimous nod in 1996. But, his victory was to be short lived as he lost his title to Pichit Cho Siriwat from Thailand before the end of the year.

His dreams of claiming a second world title were dashed in November 1997 when he was stopped in the sixth round of his WBA flyweight championship bout with Jose Bonilla while Injoo Cho, from the Republic of Korea, managed to retain his WBC super flyweight crown on points in September 1999. Although he was knocked down twice in the final round, Yamaguchi gallantly stood to hear the bell bring the bout, and the fight, to an end. In his career, Yamaguchi won 29 of his 38 fights (11 KO) while he suffered eight defeats, including five knockouts, and drew once, before he retired in 2002.

▼ Keiji Yamaguchi was born in Hokodate Japan on 17 February 1974.

Zale

Born on 29 May 1914, Anthony Florian Zaleski was universally known as the "Man of Steel" after his home town of Gary in Indiana which was a prolific steel manufacturing town. Zale was a two-time world middleweight champion, renowned for his ability to take severe punishment in the ring. His style was exciting and he was a strong body puncher who steadily wore down the opponent before knocking them out.

His first NBA middleweight championship was won on 19 July 1940, an honour he held until seven years later when he was succeeded by Rocky Graziano, while his first world title came a year later. On 28 November 1941, Zale was crowned NYSAC world middleweight champion. He held on to the title until 16 July 1947

▲ Tony Zale is hugged by his manager after knocking out Rocky Graziano.

◀ Tony Zale was renowned for being a strong body puncher.

and then reclaimed it in June 1948 with revenge against Graziano.

Zale's most prolific bouts were against the "Rock", which came over a 21-month period. The first match saw both men take a savage beating in September 1946, but Zale knocked out Graziano in the sixth round and retained his title. The three championship bouts are considered some of the most brutal and exciting in middleweight history. Zale retired after another shot at the title (this time against Marcel Cerdan in 1948) and died at his home in Chicago on 20 March 1997.

Other books also available:

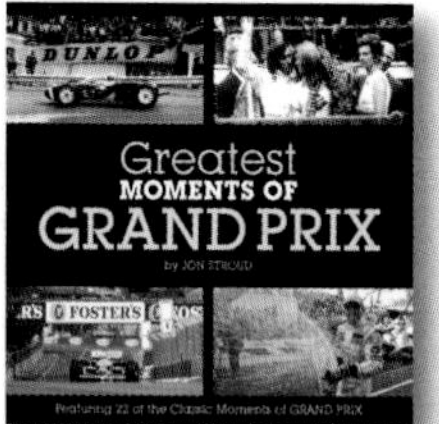

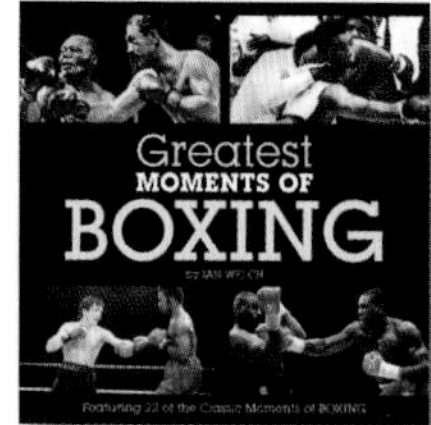

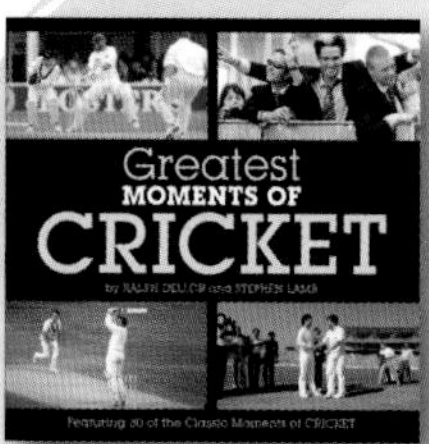

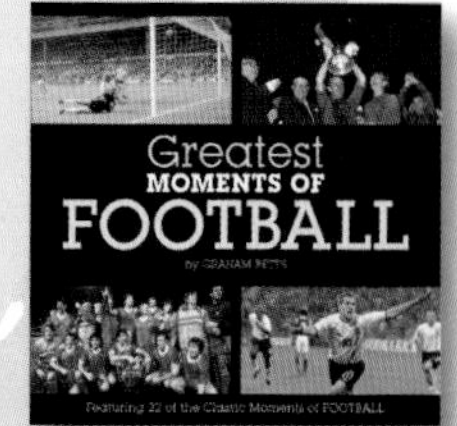

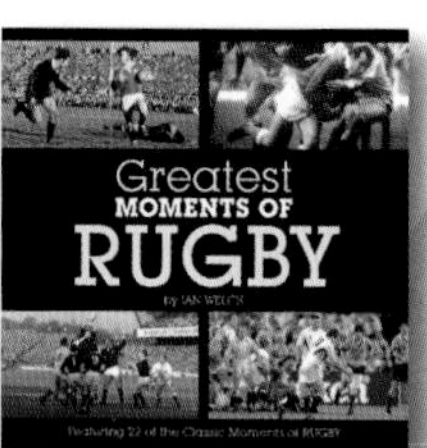

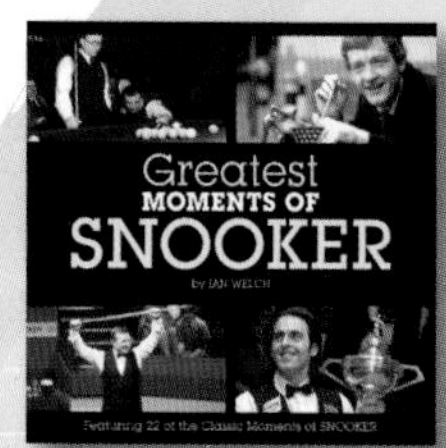

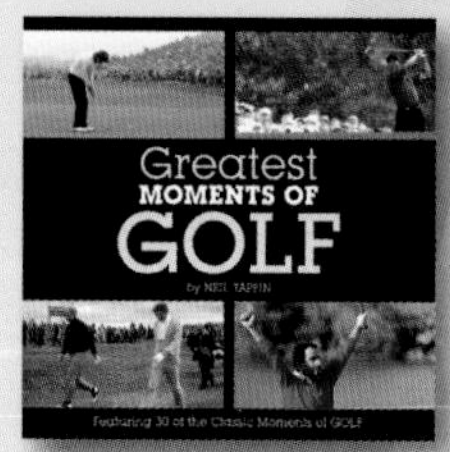

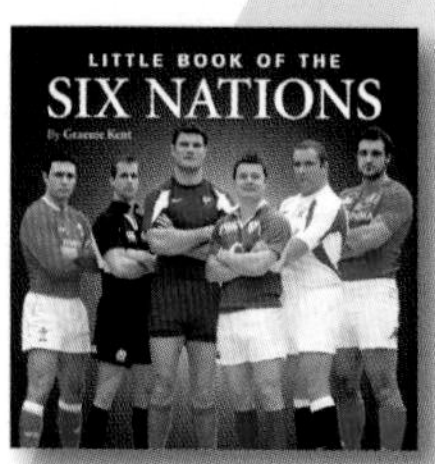

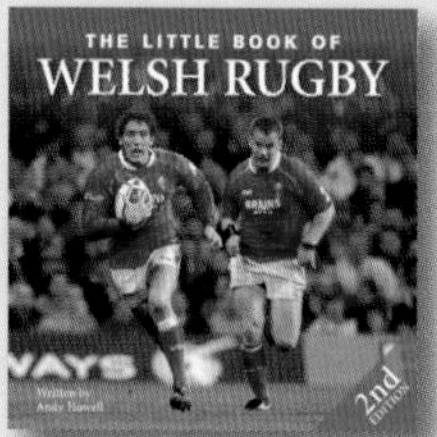

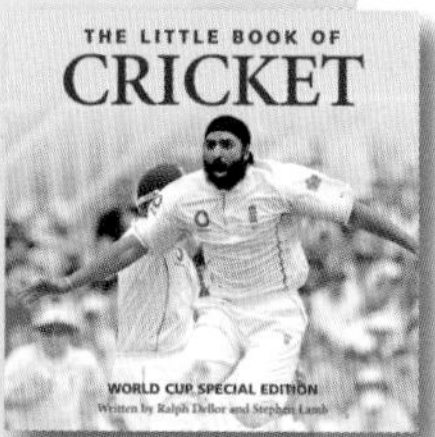

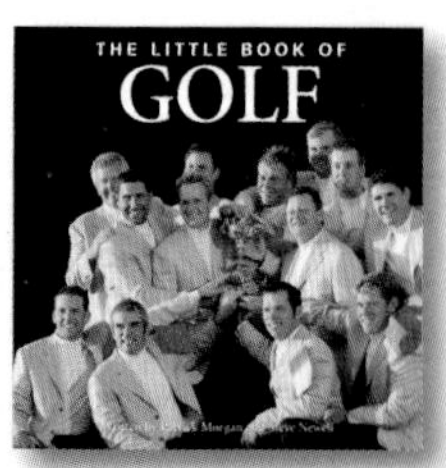

Available from all major stockists

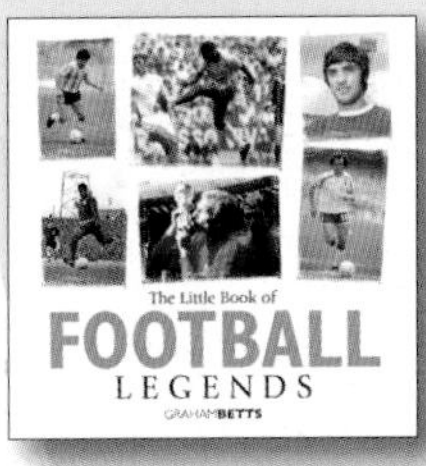

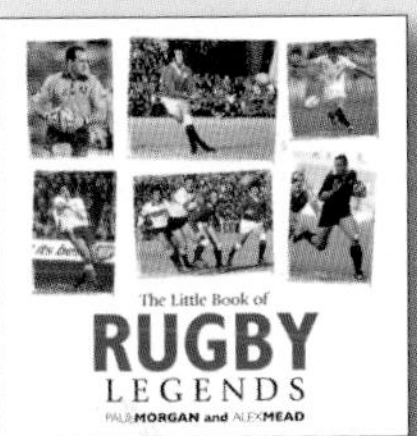

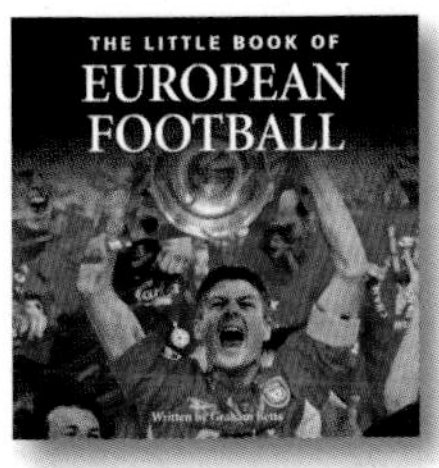

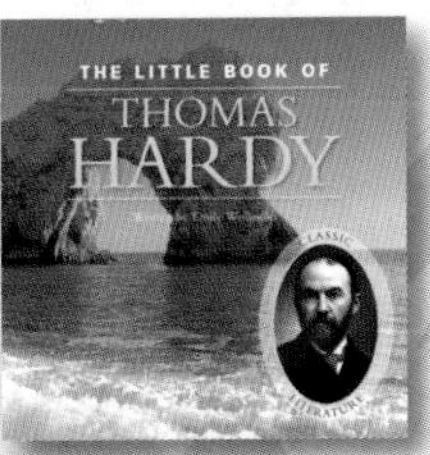

Available from all major stockists

The pictures in this book were provided courtesy of the following:

GETTY IMAGES
101 Bayham Street, London NW1 0AG

PA PHOTOS
Pavilion House, 16 Castle Boulevard, Nottingham

Creative Director: Kevin Gardner

Design and Artwork: David Wildish

Picture research: Ellie Charleston

Published by Green Umbrella Publishing

Publishers Jules Gammond and Vanessa Gardner

Written by Clyde Prisk & Lara Dearnley